50 ChatGPT Prompts to Save You 10 Hours a Week

The Everyday AI Series

Practical, fast, and accessible guides for using artificial intelligence to work smarter, think clearer, and simplify everyday life. Ready to use guides and prompts for work, home, writing and productivity.

Books in the Series:

• *Make and Master Your AI Twin* — A complete method for building, training, and aligning your personal AI assistant.

• *50 ChatGPT Prompts to Save You 10 Hours a Week* — A tactical, plug-and-play guide to eliminating daily friction with AI.

Each book is designed to be read independently or as part of a growing library of tools that help you use AI with purpose, creativity, and clarity.

50 ChatGPT Prompts to Save You 10 Hours a Week

How to Automate Your Life With AI

By Merritt Altman

Unbound Press

50 ChatGPT Prompts to Save You 10 Hours a Week: How to Automate Your Life With AI

Merritt Altman

ISBN Paperback 9798274767330/9798295432989
ISBN Hardcover 9798295433047/9798274832205
ISBN ebook 979829542996

Dedication

For everyone who feels stuck but wants to move forward. I hope this book is your first step.

"Logic is the beginning of wisdom—not the end."

—Spock

Contents

Preface

Most people approach ChatGPT out of curiosity, not strategy. They open the app, ask a question, and hope for something useful. Sometimes it works. Often it doesn't. The difference between "interesting tool" and "indispensable assistant" isn't intelligence, it's structure.

This book exists because the average person is overwhelmed, short on time, and unsure where to start with AI. They don't need a technical manual; they need a simple starting point that removes obstacles immediately. The goal isn't mastery of the model; it's mastery of the tasks that waste unnecessary time. That distinction is important.

In building this series, I kept returning to one question: What would help someone reduce their daily effort *today*? Not in theory, but in practice. Inside their inbox, their calendar, their home routines, their planning, their learning, and their decision-making. The answer isn't more information. It's better prompts, better systems, and clearer workflows.

The 50 prompts in this book are designed to give readers leverage. Each prompt is structured so anyone—regardless of experience—can copy it, paste it, and see an immediate reduction in cognitive load. These are not "creative suggestions"; they are functional templates. They turn AI into a tool that works without requiring the user to become an expert.

The purpose of this preface is simple: to tell you what this book is and what it is not.

It is not a philosophical discussion about artificial intelligence. It is not a technical guide to how language models work. It is not a collection of generic advice.

It is a field manual for removing everyday friction.

If you want a clearer mind, a lighter week, and a reliable starting point for integrating AI into your life without being overwhelmed, the next chapters provide that structure. Think of this book as a shortcut—one that turns learning into action and replaces trial-and-error with predictable results.

As Ferris Bueller once said, "Life moves pretty fast." So, let's go.

Introduction

Why Prompts Save Time and Effort

If you're using ChatGPT by typing random questions, getting random answers, and wondering why it isn't saving you any meaningful time, the answer is simple: AI won't save you time. Good prompts will.

What is a prompt? Prompts are the system that turns a general-purpose AI into a high-leverage assistant. Without structure, AI guesses what you want; with structure, it delivers exactly what you need. This book is about that structure.

When you understand how to control AI with precise, targeted prompts, you remove dozens of micro-tasks that drain your attention every day—drafting emails, sorting information, planning your week, analyzing decisions, breaking down projects, synthesizing articles, generating ideas, and more. Done manually, these tasks add up. Done well with AI, they compress hours of mental effort into minutes.

The central claim of this book is straightforward: If you use the right prompts the right way, you can reclaim 10 hours a week of time and cognitive bandwidth.

Not by working harder or being more disciplined. Instead, by systematically and repeatedly reducing the friction that slows you down every day.

What "10 Hours a Week" Actually Represents

Ten hours is not just a productivity number. It is the cumulative effect of eliminating constant, low-grade drain:

- the six emails that require too much wording
- the project you keep avoiding because it feels heavy
- the planning you never have enough energy for
- the research rabbit holes
- the rewriting, summarizing, organizing, re-organizing
- the "I'll do it later" loop

When you remove these burdens, you free up the mental space required for more meaningful work like writing, creating, learning, resting, or simply thinking clearly again.

How This Book Works

This is not a list of 50 prompts meant to be skimmed once and forgotten. Every prompt is built as a mini-system designed to be used repeatedly.

Each one includes:

- The exact prompt
- Why it works
- When to use it
- Example input & output
- Variations
- A speed tip

This format ensures you don't just copy and paste—you understand the mechanism, which makes you stronger and faster over time.

How to Use This Book Efficiently

You can read it front to back, but you don't have to. The fastest way to benefit is:

- Start with the problem you want solved today.
- Pick the corresponding prompt.
- Use the example to shape the input.
- Save any prompt that works for you and build your own library.

If you string even three or four of these prompts into a weekly routine, the time savings compound quickly.

You don't need more discipline. You need fewer friction points. The right prompts eliminate those friction points. Let's get started.

Chapter 1 — The Anatomy of a High-Performing Prompt

What a Good Prompt Does

Most people assume a prompt is just a question. It isn't. A prompt is a set of instructions that determine the quality, clarity, and usefulness of the model's response.

When a prompt is vague, ChatGPT fills in the blanks with assumptions—usually the wrong ones. When a prompt is structured, the model delivers consistent, reliable output with far less back-and-forth.

At the foundation of every effective prompt are four components that work together: role, task, constraints, and output.

1. Role tells the model who to be.

The model performs better when it understands the perspective or expertise it should adopt. A financial analyst, an editor, a meal planner, and a project manager all generate different responses—and accuracy increases when the role is explicit.

2. Task defines exactly what you want done.

Most poor outputs come from unclear or layered requests. A good task statement removes ambiguity, making it obvious what the model should focus on and what it should ignore.

3. Constraints set the boundaries: length, tone, reading level, format, exclusions, required details.

Constraints prevent drift and reduce the chance the model produces something overly long, unfocused, or off-topic. They are the guardrails that keep the output tight.

4. Output identifies the final form you want: a list, a summary, a table, a paragraph, a plan, a script, a template.

This reduces revision cycles and ensures the result is immediately usable.

When these four parts work together, the model has the information it needs to produce a high-quality result the first time. Without them, it guesses—and guessing always costs time.

Mistakes That Slow You Down
Most prompt failures come from predictable problems:

- Asking broad or multi-layered questions.

If the request contains several tasks at once, the model blends them together and dilutes the result.

- Assuming the model understands context you haven't provided.

ChatGPT doesn't know your priorities, goals, constraints, or preferences unless you spell them out.

- Skipping constraints.

Length, tone, formatting, and exclusions are what keep the output clean. Without constraints, the model tends to produce generic or excessive content.

- Requesting a type of output without defining its structure.

"Write a summary" is vague. "Write a five-sentence summary with three bullet points of key insights" is actionable.

- Letting the model determine the purpose.

If you don't specify how you intend to use the output, the model defaults to a generic response designed for broad appeal—not for your actual need.

- Revising instead of clarifying.

People often fix a bad result by asking for edits instead of improving the underlying prompt. That compounds confusion rather than resolving it.

The goal of this book is not perfection, but predictability. When you understand the role-task-constraints-output structure, the model becomes consistent, and the number of unusable responses decreases significantly. Each good prompt saves time. Each bad one creates more work.

Chapter 2 — Productivity & Focus (10 Prompts)

Most people lose time not because their work is difficult, but because the friction around their work is high.

Decision fatigue, unclear priorities, scattered tasks, mental clutter, and constant context-switching create invisible time drains that add up to hours each week. Productivity isn't just about getting more done—it's about removing the conditions that slow you down.

This chapter addresses the core bottlenecks that undermine focus: planning, prioritization, task breakdown, decision-making, email management, and the constant pressure to keep track of too much information at once. The goal is to offload the cognitive load so you can direct your attention where it actually matters.

Each prompt in this chapter functions as a structured replacement for common daily friction points. They help you clarify your day in seconds, break large projects into manageable steps, convert vague obligations into specific actions, and create an environment where deep focus is possible without relying on motivation or willpower.

The through-line is simple: when your mind is not burdened with holding and organizing everything, productivity becomes an outcome, not an effort.

1. **Daily Plan Builder**

Prompt
"Build my daily plan. Use: top 3 priorities, 2–3 supporting tasks, a realistic timeline, and one recovery block. Ask clarifying questions only if needed."

Why it works
A structured day removes the invisible friction caused by switching tasks, making decisions, and guessing what to do next. Even high performers waste hours on "in-between time," the five minutes here, the distracted wandering there, and the mental drifting between tasks. This prompt removes all of that by enforcing clarity and sequence.

The model breaks your day into a prioritized structure rather than an overwhelming to-do list. It leans into cognitive science: when tasks are arranged in a time-bound order, your brain stops renegotiating decisions and starts executing. You save energy and reduce the likelihood of procrastination.

Finally, including a "recovery block" creates sustainability. Most people plan for their ideal energy, not their real energy. This prompt accounts for the inevitable dips, interruptions, and mental drain that arise in every normal day.

When to Use It

Use this prompt anytime you feel:

- mentally scattered
- overwhelmed by competing responsibilities
- unsure where to begin
- behind schedule and need a rapid reset
- like your day "happened to you" instead of you driving it

It's especially effective:

- first thing in the morning
- after lunch when energy dips
- after unexpected disruptions
- when you only have a few hours left and need to maximize the time

The more chaotic your day feels, the more powerful this prompt becomes.

<u>Examples</u>

Example 1- Today's To-Do's

Input

Today: finish slide deck, email clients, gym, prep kids' lunches, short grocery run.

Output

8:00–10:00 Finish slide deck
10:00–10:15 Recovery block
10:15–11:00 Email clients
11:00–11:30 Kids' lunches
11:30–12:00 Grocery run
4:00–5:00 Gym

Example 2 – Feeling Overwhelmed

Input
I feel overwhelmed. Tasks: budget review, laundry, call insurance, order birthday gift, write 2 pages of my book.

Output
Top 3 Priorities: book pages, budget review, insurance call

Timeline:
9:00–9:45 Book writing
9:45–10:00 Recovery
10:00–10:20 Insurance call
10:20–11:00 Budget review
Afternoon: laundry + gift

Example 3 – Simplify My Day

Input
Just need a simple structure. Tasks: content planning, social posts, 20-minute walk.

Output

Plan:
Content planning (9:00–10:00)
Walk (10:00–10:20)
Social posts (10:20–11:00)

Variations

- Low-energy version: "Use an ultra-light plan assuming low cognitive energy."
- Aggressive version: "Plan this day assuming I'm firing on all cylinders."
- Interruptions-expected version: "Build a flexible plan with buffer blocks."

Pro Difficulty Upgrade

Ask the model to include:

- predicted obstacles
- micro-deadlines inside each block
- communication you need to send
- the "one thing" that makes the day successful even if all else fails

Example upgrade:

"Add predicted obstacles and the smallest possible version of each task."

This teaches you to plan like a chief of staff.

Common Mistakes to Avoid

- Listing 20+ tasks—you'll get a plan you can't execute.
- Leaving out personal errands—those derail the schedule later.
- Ignoring energy dips—results in unrealistic scheduling.
- Not checking the timeline the model gives you—adjust it as needed.

The goal is realism, not perfection.

Speed Tip
Paste your calendar link or drop bullet points; even better, drop in screenshots, and ChatGPT will automatically extract everything.

Template You Can Reuse
"Build my day using this structure:

- Top 3 priorities
- Supporting tasks
- Timeline with start/end
- One recovery block
- What success looks like today
- Questions only if essential

My tasks: [paste]."

2. **Weekly Planning Reset**

Prompt
"Create a weekly plan based on my goals. Include: theme of the week, 3 major outcomes, 5 key tasks, and a realistic workload distribution."

Why it Works
Most people treat each week as a carryover from the last—unfinished tasks carry over, new demands pile up, and priorities blur. This prompt breaks that cycle. It forces you to step back, reset, and intentionally shape the next seven days. Research on attentional control shows that weekly planning, not daily, is the ideal approach for strategic thinking. Daily planning is too detailed; monthly planning is too vague. Weekly planning keeps you focused.

The model also trims your ambitions into three major outcomes. This constraint is crucial. When everything is important, nothing is. By narrowing to three, you preserve bandwidth and dramatically increase the likelihood you finish meaningful work instead of drowning in low-value tasks.

Finally, the "realistic workload distribution" corrects the universal mistake: packing Monday with everything you didn't do last week. AI distributes your tasks based on actual working hours, energy patterns, and complexity. This eliminates overplanning and gives you a structure that feels achievable instead of aspirational.

When to Use It:

- Every Sunday evening or Monday morning
- When the previous week was chaotic and needs a clean break
- When you feel like you're doing "a lot" but making little progress
- After major life changes (new job, health issues, projects shifting)
- When you're juggling multiple domains—work, home, personal goals

This prompt is especially powerful:

- At the start of new quarters
- Before travel-heavy weeks
- After burnout or fatigue
- When you want to re-anchor your direction

If you're drifting, this pulls you back to intention.

<u>Examples</u>

Example 1, Plan My Week

Input
Goals: finish book chapter, organize garage, prepare for presentation.

Output
Theme: Simplify and Complete

Major Outcomes:

- Draft and edit Chapter 3
- Presentation deck completed
- Garage fully organized

Workload:
Mon–Tue: Writing
Wed: Deck prep
Thu–Fri: Garage project

Example 2, Workweek Priorities

Input
Goal is work-only: client project, internal meeting prep, clean up inbox.

Output
Theme: Clarity & Execution

Outcomes:

- Client deliverable polished
- Meeting prepared
- Inbox to zero

Tasks: drafting, reviewing notes, scheduling replies, finalizing slides

Example 3, Organize the Chaos

Input
I'm overwhelmed. Too many tasks: dentist, bills, laundry, writing outline, mom's birthday prep, meal planning.

Output
Theme: Stabilization

Outcomes:

- Personal admin cleaned up
- Outline completed
- Birthday plan finished

Variations

- Low-stress week: "Plan this as a gentle week with low expectations and lots of buffer."
- Deadline week: "Plan aggressively to meet a hard deadline."
- Mixed priorities: "Separate personal vs. professional outcomes."
- Brain fog variation: "Simplify everything to one outcome per day."

Pro Difficulty Upgrade

Add:

- capacity forecasting
- risk assessment for each outcome
- slots for communication you must send
- invisible tasks (prep, cleanup, follow-up)
- a "success metric" for the week

Example enhancement:

"Now add predicted barriers and mini-milestones for each outcome."

This teaches strategic pacing.

Common Mistakes to Avoid

- Setting vague outcomes ("work on project")
- Planning based on hope instead of hours
- Ignoring personal-life tasks that will interrupt your week
- Adding too many outcomes—this dilutes progress
- Treating every day identically despite energy fluctuations

A good week has a center of gravity, not 20 loose ends.

Template You Can Reuse

"Create a weekly plan with:

- Theme
- 3 major outcomes
- 5 key tasks
- Realistic workload distribution
- Daily focus

My goals/tasks: [paste]."

Speed Tip
If you're unsure about your outcomes, paste your cluttered to-do list. ChatGPT will automatically identify the most important items.

3. Priority Clarifier

Prompt
"I have these tasks: [paste list]. Sort them into: Must Do, Should Do, Nice to Do. Then tell me the one task with the highest leverage."

Why It Works
Decision fatigue destroys productivity. When your brain tries to handle a long list of competing tasks, it gets overwhelmed by choices instead of taking action. This approach simplifies that overwhelm by creating a tiered hierarchy, a method supported by cognitive-load research: when the mind organizes tasks into clear categories, it becomes much easier to act.

The model also identifies the most impactful task— the one action that delivers the greatest effect compared to effort. Humans tend to pick easy tasks for quick dopamine hits, even when those tasks don't significantly advance life. This prompt removes emotional bias and promotes a strategic perspective.

Finally, differentiating between Must, Should, and Nice helps avoid the common mistake of treating everything as urgent. This clears mental space, lowers stress, and speeds up meaningful progress.

When to Use It

Use this prompt when:

- You're staring at a long list and don't know where to start
- You feel overwhelmed or paralyzed
- You suspect you're doing low-value tasks while high-value tasks linger
- You're planning a day with limited time (e.g., 1–3 hours of available work)
- You're juggling work + personal responsibilities
- You want to reset priorities after interruptions, travel, or emergencies

Especially helpful:

- Mondays
- After a crisis week
- During periods of fatigue, brain fog, or mental clutter

- When working on large creative projects with many moving parts

Examples

Example 1, To-Do List

Input
Tasks: finish invoice, buy dog food, start book outline, schedule dentist, clean kitchen.

Output
Must Do: invoice, dentist, dog food
Should Do: book outline
Nice to Do: clean kitchen
Highest Leverage: finish invoice — unlocks cash flow and client satisfaction.

Example 2, To-Do List

Input
Tasks: respond to emails, update resume, send three job applications, meal prep, laundry.

Output
Must Do: job applications, update resume
Should Do: respond to emails
Nice to Do: laundry, meal prep
Highest Leverage: applications — directly moves you toward employment.

Example 3, To-Do List

Input
Tasks: write newsletter, book flights, finalize project timeline, renew car registration, return Amazon package.

Output
Must Do: renew registration (legal), finalize timeline (work-critical)
Should Do: book flights
Nice to Do: return package, write newsletter
Highest Leverage: finalize timeline — unblocks the entire project.

Variations

- Work-only version: "Sort strictly by business impact."
- Personal-life version: "Sort based on stress reduction and life maintenance."
- Emergency version: "Sort with a 1–2 hour time horizon—only what must happen today."
- Fatigue version: "Sort tasks and simplify the top three into micro-steps."

Pro Difficulty Upgrade

Ask the model to include:

- Impact vs. effort mapping (2x2 matrix)

- Dependency analysis (which tasks unlock others)
- Risk of delay (what happens if each task is postponed)
- Momentum score (what creates the biggest forward motion)

Example enhancement

"Add an impact/effort matrix and identify all high-impact/low-effort items."

This turns your task list into a strategic decision model.

Common Mistakes to Avoid

- Dumping too many ambiguous tasks—be specific
- Letting emotional discomfort push a task into "Should" instead of "Must"
- Putting creative work under "Nice" even when it fuels long-term goals
- Allowing overdue or legally-required tasks to sit in lower categories
- Confusing urgency (time-based) with importance (impact-based)

The model is only as honest as the list you provide.

Template You Can Reuse

"Sort these tasks into Must Do, Should Do, and Nice to Do. Then identify the highest-leverage task and why. Tasks: [paste]."

Speed Tip
If your list is disorganized, simply screenshot your notes app or planner and paste the text. ChatGPT will automatically extract tasks.

4. **Delegation Simulator**

Prompt
"I want to delegate more. For these tasks: [list], tell me: (1) what I can hand off, (2) who the ideal delegate is, (3) what the handoff instructions should say."

Why It Works
Most people don't delegate because they fail to see what can be handed off. Cognitive bias—especially the "false uniqueness" effect—causes us to think tasks need our personal touch when they actually don't. This prompt offers an external, objective look at what truly needs your involvement and what doesn't.

The model also identifies the ideal delegate for each task. When delegation fails, it's usually because the wrong person gets the wrong assignment. AI analyzes the nature of the task—administrative, creative, logistical, relational—and matches it to the best role or skill set. This eliminates guesswork and greatly improves the success rate of delegation.

Finally, the prompt produces handoff instructions, an area where people often struggle. Poorly defined instructions cause rework, frustration, and a lack of trust. Clear, concise handoff notes improve execution success and save hours of your time each week. Delegation then stops being a burden and instead becomes a force multiplier.

When to Use It

Use this prompt when:

- Your to-do list is too long
- You're repeating the same tasks weekly
- You're spending time on low-skill or low-leverage tasks
- You're preparing for a busy season and need more capacity
- You're a parent, partner, manager, or business owner with help available
- You feel resentful or burned out by tasks others could handle

Especially useful:

- At the start of a project (delegate setup tasks early)
- When your workload spikes unexpectedly
- Before travel

- During health issues or fatigue
- When building systems or SOPs

If you want to scale your productivity, this is one of the highest-impact prompts in the book.

<u>Examples</u>

Example 1 — Personal Life
Input
Tasks: grocery shopping, updating insurance info, decluttering the garage, sending birthday invitations.

Output
Delegate: grocery shopping → spouse/teenager
Handoff: "Buy items on this list. Stick to store brands. Text me if substitutions needed."

Delegate: birthday invitations → friend or older child
Handoff: "Use the template, confirm guest list, send by Friday."
Keep: insurance update (requires personal details)

Example 2 — Family & Home

Input
Tasks: laundry, ordering school supplies, planning meals, managing budget, deep-cleaning kitchen.

Output
Delegate: school supplies → older child
Handoff: "Buy items from this Amazon list today. Check total before ordering."

Delegate: deep-clean → cleaning service
Handoff: "Kitchen deep clean: inside microwave, backsplash, stove, counters."

Keep: budget management (sensitive financial info)

Example 3 — Work / Business

Input
Tasks: create slide template, research competitors, write proposal, schedule meetings, summarize feedback.

Output
Delegate: competitor research → assistant
Handoff: "Find top 5 competitors. Capture pricing, features, pros/cons. One-page summary."

Delegate: scheduling → admin
Handoff: "Find a 30-minute window that works for all attendees. Confirm and send agenda."
Keep: writing proposal (high-leverage, strategic)

Variations

- Work-only version: “Sort strictly based on professional roles.”
- Household version: “Delegate among spouse, kids, or services.”
- Small-business version: “Assign tasks across team roles: marketing, admin, operations.”
- Zero-budget version: “Delegate only to family or coworkers—no pay-required options.”
- Mental fatigue version: “Highlight the easiest tasks to hand off immediately.”

Pro Difficulty Upgrade

Ask the model to include:

- task frequency (weekly, monthly, quarterly)
- suggested automations (e.g., subscriptions, AI tools)
- “minimum instructions required” version
- whether the task needs a SOP
- risk rating for delegating incorrectly
- whether this should be delegated permanently or temporarily

Example enhancement:

“Add: recommended automation tools, SOP suggestions, and the minimum viable instruction set.”

This helps you scale like a manager, not a solo operator.

Common Mistakes to Avoid

- Thinking delegation means losing control
- Delegating unclear tasks (clarity first, then handoff)
- Giving vague instructions ("Just handle it")
- Delegating emotionally-charged tasks (usually backfires)
- Assigning tasks to the wrong skill set
- Re-checking work excessively (defeats the purpose)

Delegation is a skill; precision makes it successful.

Template You Can Reuse
"Evaluate these tasks and tell me: what can be delegated, who the ideal delegate is, the exact handoff instructions. Tasks: [paste]."

Speed Tip: If you're unsure who can take tasks, simply say:

"Assign these to typical household/work roles."
AI will distribute tasks intelligently across spouse, teen, assistant, contractor, or coworker.

5. **Fifteen-Minute Focus Booster**

Prompt

"Turn this task into a simple 15-minute sprint with micro-steps: [task]. Remove complexity."

Why It Works

Most procrastination isn't about laziness—it's caused by cognitive overload. When a task seems too big, too vague, or too mentally taxing, the brain resists starting. This approach tackles that hesitation directly by breaking the task into tiny, easy micro-steps that can be done in just 15 minutes.

The magic is in the micro-step breakdown. Instead of "write chapter," you get "open document," "write working title," "brain-dump 3 ideas," "expand one idea into 3 sentences." Each one is easy. This activates the Zeigarnik effect—once you begin, your brain wants to keep going. Momentum replaces resistance.

The 15-minute limit is also psychologically powerful. A short, timed session feels safe; even tough tasks become manageable. Most people find that once they start, 15 minutes turns into 30 or 45 because the energy needed to begin is no longer a barrier.

When to Use It

Use this prompt when:

- You keep putting off a specific task

- A project feels too big to start
- You feel mentally foggy or overwhelmed
- You have a small window of time and want to make progress
- You need to reclaim momentum after a slump
- You're dealing with perfectionism
- You want a quick win that jumpstarts your day

It's especially effective:

- During low-energy periods
- Immediately after interruptions
- On tasks you've been avoiding for days or weeks
- When facing emotionally heavy tasks (emails, paperwork, cleanup)
- At the beginning of large creative projects

If you can't start, this prompt gets you moving.

<u>Examples</u>

Example 1 — Writing Task

Input
Task: Write the first page of my chapter.

Output

- Open your writing app
- Title the document (working title only)

- Write one sentence describing the chapter's purpose
- List 3 bullet points you want to cover
- Turn each bullet into one sentence
- Expand sentences into 2–3 lines
- Read once, no edits

Total time: 15 minutes

Outcome: The skeleton of the page exists—momentum unlocked.

Example 2 — Messy Chore

Input
Task: Clean the garage.

Output

- Set a timer for 15 minutes
- Grab one trash bag
- Choose one small area (don't scan the whole room)
- Toss obvious trash
- Group similar items together
- Put 5 things in their proper place
- Take out the trash bag

Total time: 15 minutes

Outcome: Visible progress without overwhelm.

Example 3 — Administrative Task

Input
Task: Call insurance and request updated card.

Output

- Find the customer service number
- Copy/paste it into your phone
- Write the 1-sentence script
- Call
- Save confirmation number
- Set reminder to check for email arrival

Total time: 15 minutes

Outcome: Task is done—no more mental weight.

Variations

- 5-minute starter: "Give me a 5-minute version to break resistance."
- Brain fog mode: "Make the steps ultra-simple—assume low capacity."
- Aggressive version: "Create a faster-paced, high-intensity 15-minute sprint."
- Creative block version: "Make steps that unlock creativity first."
- Delegation version: "Turn this 15-minute sprint into a handoff task someone else can do."

Pro Difficulty Upgrade

Ask the model to include:

- micro-rewards (tiny positive reinforcement after completion)
- the “minimum viable version” of the task
- predicted obstacles and fast bypasses
- a 15-minute follow-up plan if momentum continues
- emotional reframes (“This is small. This is doable.”)

Example enhancement:

“Add predicted blockers and the tiniest possible version of each micro-step.”

This permanently improves your task activation habits.

Common Mistakes to Avoid

- Trying to do the whole project in 15 minutes
- Adding steps that require decisions (keep them automatic)
- Letting perfection creep in
- Turning the sprint into planning instead of action
- Treating 15 minutes as trivial—consistent short blocks build entire books

Remember: the goal is start, not finish.

Template You Can Reuse
"Turn this task into a 15-minute micro-step sprint. Keep steps tiny and sequential. Task: [paste]."

Speed Tip: If you're stuck and don't know why, add: "Tell me why I'm resisting this task in one sentence."

This surfaces the friction instantly.

6. **Decision Helper**

Prompt
"Help me make a decision. Summarize the options, risks, and likely outcomes using a simple 3-box model: Choice, Why Choose It, What Could Go Wrong."

Why It Works
Most decisions are hard not because the options are unclear but because the mental model is unclear. When your brain tries to weigh many factors—risk, timing, benefits, emotional costs—it quickly becomes overwhelmed. This overload causes indecision, procrastination, or impulsive choices that feel good now but don't match long-term goals.

This prompt works because it simplifies all the complexity into a three-box structure—Choice,

Why Choose It, and What Could Go Wrong. This straightforward framework reflects how executive decision-making is taught: identify the options, explain the reasoning, and outline the risks. When these are clear, the best option becomes usually obvious.

The model also removes emotional noise. Humans tend to overweight fear, discomfort, and anxiety when making decisions. AI presents each option with calm clarity, helping you evaluate choices logically instead of impulsively. The result is a clearer decision process—and a faster one.

When to Use It

Use this prompt when:

- You feel stuck between two or more options
- You've been delaying a decision for days or weeks
- You're spinning in mental circles
- You keep changing your mind
- You're afraid of making the "wrong" call
- You want a neutral, objective breakdown

It's especially effective for:

- Career choices (projects, jobs, clients, timing)
- Creative and business decisions (book topics, launches, priorities)

- Personal choices (home repairs, purchases, scheduling)
- Emotional decisions you want to evaluate with clarity
- Choices with long-term consequences

If your mind feels foggy, anxious, or conflicted, this prompt brings order.

<u>Examples</u>

Example 1 — Career

Input
Decision: Should I take the new job or stay where I am?

Output
Choice: Take new job
- Why Choose It: higher pay, new skills, growth environment
- What Could Go Wrong: culture mismatch, longer commute

Choice: Stay
- Why Choose It: stability, known environment
- What Could Go Wrong: stagnation, missed opportunity

Example 2 — Home Life

Input
Decision: Repair my old laptop or buy a new one?

Output
Choice: Repair

- Why Choose It: cheaper short-term
- What Could Go Wrong: breaks again soon

Choice: Buy new

- Why Choose It: long-term stability
- What Could Go Wrong: higher upfront cost

Example 3 — Project Workflow

Input
Decision: Should I outline the whole book first or write chapter-by-chapter?

Output
Choice: Outline first

- Why Choose It: strong structure, easier editing
- What Could Go Wrong: feels slow at the start

Choice: Write chapter-by-chapter

- Why Choose It: more creative flow
- What Could Go Wrong: risk of major rewrites

Variations

- Two-choice version: “Compare just A vs. B.”
- Three-option version: “Include a third alternative I’m overlooking.”
- Gut-check version: “Tell me what choice aligns most with my long-term goals.”
- Risk-tolerance version: “Recommend based on a low-risk or high-risk preference.”
- Emotional version: “Show me the emotional costs and benefits per option.”

Pro Difficulty Upgrade

Ask the model to add:

- Likelihood rating for each outcome (high/medium/low)
- Severity score for each risk
- What decision will you regret least in 5 years?
- Hidden third or fourth options you didn’t consider
- Upside potential vs. downside risk
- Decision-making heuristics (“If X, then Y”)

Example enhancement:

“Add likelihood and impact scores, then recommend the option with the best risk-adjusted upside.”

This teaches you executive-level decision thinking.

Common Mistakes to Avoid

- Asking the AI which option you "should" choose—own your decision
- Providing vague inputs
- Hiding emotional preferences
- Letting sunk costs influence the choice
- Treating all risks as equal
- Seeking perfection instead of clarity

The goal is clarity, not certainty.

Template You Can Reuse

"Help me make a decision using the 3-box model: Choice, Why Choose It, What Could Go Wrong. Decision: [paste]."

Speed Tip

"Tell me the smallest next step that would help me decide."

This breaks the paralysis immediately.

7. **Email Triage**

Prompt
"Turn these emails into a triage table with: Reply Now, Reply Today, Reply Later, Ignore/Delete. [paste emails]"

Why It Works
Email overwhelm is one of the largest silent productivity drains. Most inboxes are an unorganized jumble of requests, questions, reminders, opportunities, and noise. When everything seems equally urgent, you burn energy deciding what needs your attention. Most of the lost time happens not in writing replies but in sorting priorities.

This prompt addresses that by turning your cluttered inbox into a structured decision table.

Instead of repeatedly scanning emails, your brain gets a clear map of what needs immediate action and what can wait. The act of triaging emails—long recognized in emergency medicine and military operations as life-saving—applies just as effectively to managing cognitive workload.

It also helps eliminate guilt- or anxiety-driven decision-making. Many people feel pressure to respond immediately to everything. With AI categorizing messages, you regain control, lower emotional stress, and react strategically instead of impulsively.

When to Use It

Use this prompt when:

- Your inbox feels out of control
- You have unread or unanswered messages piling up
- You don't know where to start
- You feel overwhelmed or stressed just looking at your inbox
- You want to clear backlog quickly
- You need to prepare for time away (vacation, travel, deep work days)

It is especially effective:

- After weekends or holidays
- Once a week as a reset
- During busy project seasons

- When you're expecting important communication and don't want to miss it

This turns your inbox from a source of stress into a manageable workflow.

<u>Examples</u>

Example 1 — Work Inbox

Input

- Client asking for updated proposal
- HR asking for annual forms
- Newsletter subscription
- Friend sharing a meme
- Team asking for feedback on draft

Output

Reply Now: client proposal
Reply Today: team draft feedback, HR forms
Reply Later: friend meme
Ignore/Delete: newsletter

Example 2 — Personal Inbox

Input

- Dentist reminder
- Amazon shipping notice
- School asking for field trip chaperone
- Promo email
- HOA meeting summary

Output
Reply Now: school chaperone response
Reply Today: dentist confirmation
Reply Later: HOA notes
Ignore/Delete: promo email, shipping notice

Example 3 — Mixed Responsibilities

Input

- Editor asking for revision timeline
- Kid's teacher asking a question
- Bank fraud alert
- Newsletter from a podcast
- PTA fundraiser message

Output

- Reply Now: bank alert, teacher
- Reply Today: editor
- Reply Later: PTA
- Ignore/Delete: podcast email

Variations

- Work-only: "Categorize based strictly on business priority."
- Low-energy: "Give me just the three messages that need action today."
- Executive version: "Sort emails by strategic impact rather than urgency."
- Spam-heavy inbox: "Separate true spam from ignorable-but-legitimate messages."

Pro Difficulty Upgrade

Ask the model to add:

- reasons each email belongs in that category
- the draft replies for the "Reply Now" items
- subject line summaries
- estimated time to respond to each
- emotional weight indicator (stressful / neutral / easy)
- reminders or follow-up flags

Example enhancement:

"Now write draft replies for everything in the Reply Now and Reply Today categories."

This turns AI into your personal email assistant.

Common Mistakes to Avoid

- Trying to reply to everything at once
- Letting low-value emails consume mental space
- Feeling obligated to answer all messages
- Using the inbox as a task list
- Not archiving or deleting noise
- Avoiding high-stakes emails, creating anxiety loops

Your inbox should serve you—not the other way around.

Template You Can Reuse
"Sort these emails into: Reply Now, Reply Today, Reply Later, and Ignore/Delete.
Emails: [paste]."

Speed Tip: You can paste entire email threads, screenshots, or raw text—the model will parse them automatically and identify the important parts.

8. Meeting Synthesis

Prompt
"Summarize this meeting into: key decisions, owners, deadlines, and one-sentence next steps. [paste notes]"

Why It Works
Meetings fail not because people don't talk, but because no one captures the decision structure that emerges. A typical meeting produces ideas, discussions, opinions, concerns, and partial agreements—yet unless the outcomes are organized into a clear plan, people leave with different understandings of what took place.

This prompt addresses that by transforming chaotic or lengthy meeting notes into a concise, functional summary: decisions, owners, deadlines, and next steps. That's how high-performing teams operate. Clear summaries lessen follow-up confusion, prevent rework, eliminate ambiguity, and promote accountability. It's the difference between a meeting that moves things forward and one that stalls progress.

Additionally, AI has no emotional stake in the meeting. It doesn't worry about offending others or reading between the lines. It identifies what was actually decided—rather than what people implied or hoped. This provides a neutral, dependable view of your obligations and next steps.

When to Use It

Use this prompt:

- After any meeting where multiple people discussed tasks or decisions
- When notes are messy, incomplete, or overwhelming
- When you joined late or left early and need clarity
- When you're forwarding notes to someone who wasn't there
- When multiple projects or people were involved
- For recurring meetings to track progress over time

It's especially helpful for:

- Steering committees
- Team check-ins
- One-on-one meetings
- Project kickoffs
- Strategy sessions
- Family planning or household logistics

If your meetings result in confusion or follow-up slack messages, use this.

<u>Examples</u>

Example 1 — Work / Project

Input
Notes: Discussed marketing launch. Need landing page copy. Sarah handling social posts. Deadline next Friday. Budget approved for ads. Next meeting Monday.

Output

- Decisions: run ad campaign; build landing page; launch next Friday
- Owners: landing page – Alex; social – Sarah; ads – Finance
- Deadlines: all assets by Thursday; launch Friday
- Next Step: Alex drafts landing page copy by end of day.

Example 2 — Family / Home

Input
Notes: Plan vacation. Kids want beach. Budget discussed. Need to book hotel. Check flights. Mom will research resorts.

Output

- Decisions: beach vacation approved
- Owners: resort research – Mom; flights – you
- Deadlines: pick resort by Wednesday; book everything by Friday
- Next Step: Mom sends top 3 resort options.

Example 3 — Creative Collaboration

Input
Notes: Book outline meeting. Need chapter order finalized. Remove chapter 7. Expand chapter 3. Add case study. Next call Friday.

Output

- Decisions: remove ch. 7; expand ch. 3; add case study
- Owners: chapter order – You; case study – Co-writer
- Deadlines: updated outline by Thursday
- Next Step: Draft updated outline and send for review.

Variations

- Executive version: "Prioritize decisions with revenue or impact implications."
- Mental fatigue version: "Keep summary ultra-simple with only 3 bullets."
- Team version: "Add follow-up questions to clarify loose ends."
- Conflict-heavy meeting: "Flag unresolved disagreements and propose options."
- Recurring meeting: "Track progress vs. last week's decisions."

Pro Difficulty Upgrade

Ask the model to include:

- risks if deadlines are missed
- dependencies between tasks
- time estimates for each action
- escalation points (who gets notified if blocked)
- communication drafts for follow-up
- dashboard-ready summary for project tools

Example enhancement:

"Now add risks, dependencies, and a Slack-ready update summary."

This transforms your meeting notes into a project management artifact.

Common Mistakes to Avoid

- Leaving meetings without written next steps
- Using vague owners ("team," "we," "marketing")
- Assuming everyone leaves with the same interpretation
- Forgetting to assign deadlines
- Overdocumenting and drowning in notes

Meetings are only valuable when turned into action.

Template You Can Reuse
"Summarize this meeting into:
- Key decisions
- Owners
- Deadlines
- One-sentence next step
- Notes: [paste]."

Speed Tip: If your notes are barely readable or you didn't take any, paste whatever scraps you have—even a transcript chunk or bullet list. AI will reconstruct a clean summary with surprising accuracy.

9. **Task Breakdown (Make This Simple for My Brain)**

Prompt

"Break this overwhelming task into micro-steps that require minimal cognitive load. Keep every step simple and small. Task: [task]."

Why It Works

Overwhelm stems from ambiguity. When a task is too large, unclear, or emotionally intense, your brain struggles to find a clear way forward—so it stalls. This is cognitive overload, not a character flaw. The mind avoids what it cannot visualize.

This prompt reduces overwhelm by breaking down a big, intimidating task into a clear sequence of small steps, each simple enough to feel immediately achievable. Instead of "organize the house," you get: "Pick one drawer. Empty it. Toss trash. Sort items. Wipe drawer. Put back only essentials." You shift from feeling stuck to making progress.

Humans are momentum-driven beings. When you take a small step—like opening a document, finding a phone number, or choosing a folder—your brain releases dopamine and encourages you to keep going. Momentum takes over where dread might have been. This prompt generates that momentum instantly, even when your energy or motivation is low.

When to Use It

Use this prompt when:

- You're staring at a task you've avoided
- You don't know where to start
- You feel mentally foggy, tired, or scattered
- A project feels too large to fit in your brain
- You're procrastinating despite wanting to complete the task
- You need to convert intentions into execution
- You feel intimidated or emotionally weighted by a task

It's especially powerful for:

- Creative work (writing, designing, planning)
- Administrative tasks (calling insurance, paperwork, taxes)
- Organizing and decluttering
- Financial tasks
- Conversations you're avoiding
- Anything that induces stress or perfectionism

Any task you can't start becomes doable once it's broken down enough.

<u>Examples</u>

Example 1 — Writing

Input
Task: Write a 1,000-word article.

Output

- Open your writing document
- Write a working title
- List 3 major points
- Write one sentence under each point
- Expand each sentence into 3–4 lines
- Add a quick intro paragraph
- Add a closing paragraph
- Do a light read-through (no heavy edits)

Example 2 — Home Organization

Input
Task: Clean the whole kitchen.

Output:

- Set a 10-minute timer
- Clear the sink
- Load dishwasher
- Wipe counters
- Sweep floor under island only
- Put away 5 items on counters
- Take out trash

Example 3 — Business Task
Input
Task: Prepare for client strategy meeting.

Output:

- Locate last meeting notes

- Highlight major decisions
- List 3 goals for upcoming meeting
- Draft 5 bullet talking points
- Gather any documents needed
- Send agenda to client

Variations

- Mental fatigue version: "Make steps extremely tiny—assume minimal brain capacity."
- High focus version: "Make the steps slightly larger and faster-paced."
- Emergency version: "Make a bare-minimum breakdown to move the task forward quickly."
- Creative block version: "Start with mind-unlocking steps (e.g., freewrite, brainstorm)."
- Delegation version: "Convert these micro-steps into tasks someone else can do."

Pro Difficulty Upgrade

Ask the model to include:

- estimated time for each step
- an emotional friction rating (what might feel hard)
- the minimum viable version (the smallest version that counts as done)
- obstacles you might encounter and fast bypasses

- a 5-minute “momentum extender” if you feel motivated after finishing

Example enhancement:

“Add time estimates and the bare-minimum version so I can choose between full and minimum effort.”

This trains you to scope tasks like a project manager.

Common Mistakes to Avoid

- Starting with too big a step (“write chapter”)
- Turning steps into decisions, which increases friction
- Trying to finish the whole task in one go
- Skipping micro-steps because they feel “too small”
- Letting perfectionism creep into early steps
- Creating steps that require willpower instead of clarity

The smaller the step, the easier the start. The start is everything.

Template You Can Reuse
“Break this overwhelming task into tiny, sequential micro-steps requiring minimal cognitive load. Task: [paste].”

Speed Tip: If you're overwhelmed and can't even describe the task, just write: "I'm stuck. Help me define the task."

The model will extract clarity from whatever partial thoughts you give it.

10. Energy-Aware Schedule Optimizer

Prompt
"Using my energy pattern (high: morning; medium: afternoon; low: evening), schedule my tasks so they match my energy levels. Tasks: [list]."

Why It Works
Traditional planning assumes your energy stays constant throughout the day, which is biologically false. Cognitive research shows that humans go through predictable energy peaks and dips, and productivity improves significantly when tasks are aligned with those energy patterns. High-energy periods are ideal for deep work, while low-energy times are better suited for admin, chores, or recovery.

This prompt leverages your personal rhythm—morning person, night owl, post-lunch dip, chronic fatigue periods—to build a schedule that feels natural instead of forced. When your tasks align with your biology, resistance drops. You stop fighting your body and begin cooperating with it.

For anyone managing inconsistent energy due to illness, caregiving, stress, ADHD, autoimmune conditions, or similar challenges, this is essential. The model eliminates guilt, self-judgment, and unrealistic expectations. You get a plan that's practical and sustainable, not one that falls apart under the weight of optimism.

When to Use It

Use this prompt when:

- You feel tired before the day even starts
- You've been forcing high-focus work at the wrong time
- You want to stop burning out on tasks that require more energy than you have
- You need to pace yourself due to chronic illness, fatigue, or stress
- You keep missing goals because your plan doesn't match your capacity
- You want a more humane, sustainable, low-friction way to work
- You're about to plan a heavy day and want to avoid failure cycles

Especially powerful during:

- Creative projects
- Administrative-heavy days

- High-stakes work
- Flare-ups
- Travel or disrupted routines

This turns your day into something your brain and body can actually execute.

Examples

Example 1 — Standard Workday

Input
Energy: morning high, afternoon medium, evening low

Tasks: presentation prep, dishes, emails, grocery run, budget review

Output

- High energy (8–11): presentation prep
- Medium (12–3): budget review, emails
- Low (4–6): dishes, grocery run

Example 2 — Low-Energy Day

Input
Energy: high 9–10am, medium 11–1, low the rest
Tasks: outline chapter, reply to 15 emails, fold laundry, pay bills

Output

- High energy: outline chapter (30–45 minutes only)
- Medium: pay bills, reply to 5 emails
- Low: reply to remaining emails, laundry

Example 3 — Household/Family Mix

Input
Energy: high morning, medium late afternoon, low early evening
Tasks: kids' school forms, gym, meal prep, finalize work report, return package

Output
- High: work report
- Medium: school forms, gym
- Low: meal prep, return package

Variations
- Chronic illness version: "Design for fluctuating capacity and build-in pacing blocks."
- Caregiver version: "Factor in interruptions and create highly flexible structure."
- Creative version: "Put deep creative work only in high-energy windows."
- Admin-heavy version: "Distribute low-value tasks into low-energy periods."
- Weekend version: "Design a balanced, restorative weekend plan."

Pro Difficulty Upgrade

Ask the model to include:

- predicted energy dips and spikes
- built-in buffer zones
- alternate plans if energy crashes
- a "minimum viable day" version
- a "stretch goal" version for high-energy days
- pacing strategies (Pomodoro, energy cycling, micro-breaks)
- which tasks to postpone if needed

Example enhancement:

"Add a pacing plan and minimum-viable version of today's schedule in case my energy drops."

This produces a resilient, adaptable plan instead of a fragile one.

Common Mistakes to Avoid

- Planning based on who you want to be, not who you are
- Putting hard tasks in low-energy windows
- Treating high-energy windows as infinite
- Forgetting breaks (leads to an energy crash later)
- Mixing focus tasks and admin tasks in the same block

- Assuming willpower can override physiology

Match the task to the energy—not the other way around.

Template You Can Reuse
"Using my energy pattern (high: [define], medium: [define], low: [define]), plan my tasks so each is placed in the right window. Create a realistic, time-bound schedule with buffer blocks. Tasks: [paste]."

Speed Tip
If you don't know your energy pattern, add:

"Help me identify my daily energy rhythm based on my schedule and symptoms."

The model will infer it from your lifestyle.

Chapter 3 — Communication & Writing (10 Prompts)

Communication is one of the most time-consuming parts of modern life. Writing emails, summarizing information, preparing presentations, rewriting unclear messages, and creating content can take hours—even for experienced communicators.

Most of that time isn't spent actually writing; it's spent thinking, deciding, rewriting, and finding the right tone.

This section removes friction from every form of communication.

These prompts give you:

- faster drafting
- clearer expression
- instant tone shifts
- clean summaries
- better structure
- emotional intelligence support for difficult conversations

You'll save time not by writing faster, but by letting AI handle the translation, structure, and wording so you can focus on the message.

11. Email Reply Drafting

Prompt
"Draft a clean, concise email reply based on the message below. Preserve my tone. Include 2–3 tone options if relevant. Message: [paste email]."

Why It Works
Email replies often take longer than they should because people get stuck on tone, clarity, and structure. Should you sound warm or formal? Direct or gentle? Short or detailed? Address every point or just the main ones? This decision-making process is what causes delays—even when the actual message is simple.

This prompt removes that mental block by generating a ready-to-send reply that is clear, respectful, and well-structured. The model can summarize long incoming emails into the key points, then craft a response that addresses those points effectively. It prevents you from overwriting or under-explaining—a common time sink.

Providing multiple tone options gives you control without the emotional effort of writing from scratch. You can select the version that matches your relationship with the sender or mix elements from each. The result: quicker responses, fewer misunderstandings, and a more consistent professional tone.

When to Use It

Use this prompt when:

- You're staring at an email and don't know what to say
- The email is long, emotional, confusing, or poorly written
- You want to sound polished but don't have the energy
- You're writing to someone important (boss, client, vendor, author, partner)
- You need to stay calm and diplomatic
- You want to save mental bandwidth by outsourcing the wording

It's especially useful for:

- High-stakes or uncomfortable conversations
- Customer or client communication
- Administrative responses
- Scheduling replies
- Email backlog cleanouts
- Requests you want to decline politely

If your inbox stresses you out, this prompt will change your life.

<u>Examples</u>

Example 1 — Professional Email

Input
Message: "Can you send the updated proposal by Thursday? Also, did you see my question about the budget?"

Output
Neutral:
Hi [Name],
Yes—I'll have the updated proposal to you by Thursday. I also saw your budget question and will include that clarification in the revised version.
Best, [You]

Warm:
Hi [Name],
Absolutely—I'll get the updated proposal to you by Thursday and will address the budget question in the revisions.
Thanks! [You]

Example 2 — Personal Email

Input
Message: "Are you available to help with the school fundraiser this weekend?"

Output
Direct:
Hi [Name],
Thanks for reaching out. I'm not available this weekend, but I appreciate you thinking of me.

Best, [You]

Warm:
Hi [Name],
Thanks so much for asking! I'm unfortunately not able to help this weekend, but please keep me in the loop for future events.
Warmly, [You]

Example 3 — Complicated Email

Input
Message: A long message with multiple questions, complaints, or unclear structure.

Output
Hi [Name],
Thanks for the detailed note. Here are the answers to your questions:

If I missed anything, feel free to let me know.
Best, [You]

Variations

- Ultra-short version: "Write a reply under 40 words."
- Executive-friendly version: "Write a direct, concise, no-fluff reply suitable for senior leadership."
- Empathy version: "Make the reply gentle and validating."

- Boundary-setting: “Write a kind reply that says no without over-explaining.”
- Clarification request: “Reply with 3 clarifying questions instead of a full answer.”

Pro Difficulty Upgrade

Ask the model to include:

- a summary of the incoming email first
- the emotional tone of the sender
- the hidden subtext or implied requests
- risks (tone pitfalls, misinterpretations)
- three draft options: short, medium, more detailed
- suggestions for follow-up

Example enhancement:

“First summarize their email in 3 bullets, then draft replies in formal, warm, and neutral tones.”

This turns AI into your communication aide.

Common Mistakes to Avoid

- Over-apologizing (AI can help you tighten)
- Writing emotionally before cooling down
- Over-explaining—long emails create more questions

- Using vague commitments ("I'll get to it later")
- Ignoring the emotional tone of the sender
- Responding to the wrong part of the email

Let AI handle clarity. You focus on intention.

Template You Can Reuse
"Draft a clean reply to the message below. Include tone options if relevant. Keep it concise. Message: [paste]."

Speed Tip
If you paste multiple emails at once, add: "Write replies for each in separate sections."

The model will batch-process your entire inbox.

12. Rewrite for Tone

Prompt
"Rewrite this message in three tones: (1) professional, (2) warm, (3) direct. [text]"

Why It Works
Tone is one of the hardest aspects of writing because people often overcorrect. When trying to sound polite, you might become vague. When aiming to be firm, you could come across as harsh. When attempting to be friendly, you might lose clarity. This prompt removes that challenge by

creating multiple tone-adjusted versions of your message that keep your intent intact while changing the delivery.

It also gives you contrast. Seeing your message expressed three different ways helps you quickly identify which tone suits the situation—formal for clients, warm for peers, direct for problem-solving, etc. Over time, this develops intuitive tone-adjustment skills, enhancing communication in all areas of your life.

Finally, the prompt saves a lot of time. Instead of editing your words repeatedly, the model generates clean, ready-to-send versions instantly. You focus your energy on choosing, not rewriting.

When to Use It

Use this prompt when:

- You're unsure how to strike the right tone
- You need different versions for different audiences
- Your message is emotionally sensitive or high-stakes
- You want to avoid sounding rude, passive-aggressive, or overly soft
- You're emailing someone senior or unfamiliar
- You're writing customer or client communication

- You want your message to land cleanly the first time

Especially useful for:

- Apologies
- Boundary-setting
- Clarifying misunderstandings
- Requests
- Feedback
- Declining something gracefully

Anytime tone matters, this prompt removes the guesswork.

<u>Examples</u>

Example 1 — Deadline Request

Input
"Can you send me the draft by Friday?"

Output
Professional: Could you please send me the draft by Friday so we can stay on schedule?

Warm: Hey! Just checking in—would you be able to send the draft over by Friday?

Direct: Please send the draft by Friday.

Example 2 — Declining a Request

Input
"I can't take on the extra project right now."

Output
Professional: I appreciate the opportunity, but I'm unable to take on an additional project at this time.

Warm: Thank you for thinking of me! I'm pretty booked right now, so I won't be able to take this one on.

Direct: I'm not able to take on another project right now.

Example 3 — Correcting a Misunderstanding

Input
"That wasn't what we agreed on."

Output
Professional: I believe there may be a misunderstanding. Here is what we agreed on: ___

Warm: I think we may have interpreted our plan differently. My understanding was: ___

Direct: That doesn't match what we agreed on. Here's the original plan: ___

Variations

- Add “reassuring” tone: “Rewrite in warm, direct, and reassuring tones.”
- Add “motivating” tone: useful for team communication.
- Add “firm but polite” tone: ideal for boundaries.
- Add “executive” tone: clear, concise, authoritative.
- Add “apology” tone: softened wording with accountability.
- Add “enthusiastic” tone: for marketing or announcements.

Pro Difficulty Upgrade

Ask the model to include:

- tone analysis of your original message
- a recommendation: which tone best fits the situation
- explanations of how each tone adjusts the emotional impact
- risk flags (e.g., your message might sound passive, cold, or blunt)
- a fourth tone: “empathetic but firm”

Example enhancement:

“Analyze my original tone first, then rewrite in three tones and recommend the best fit.”

This elevates your tone awareness and communication precision.

Common Mistakes to Avoid

- Trying to pack too much meaning into tone
- Using warm tone when professionalism is expected
- Using direct tone when sensitivity is needed
- Apologizing excessively in professional communication
- Choosing tone based on emotion rather than goal
- Softening the message so much that clarity is lost

Let tone serve the intention—not overshadow it.

Template You Can Reuse
"Rewrite this message in professional, warm, and direct tones. Keep meaning the same. Text: [paste]."

Speed Tip
Add: "Highlight any parts of my original message that may sound harsh, unclear, or overly casual."

This gives you tone coaching as well as rewrites.

13. Clear, Concise Rewrite

Prompt
"Rewrite this so it's shorter, clearer, and easier to understand without losing meaning. [text]"

Why It Works
Most writing gets bloated because the brain drafts in thought order, not in the order the reader needs. We write how we think—circling around ideas, repeating ourselves, adding unnecessary introductions, over-explaining, or overcomplicating simple points. This makes messages longer, harder to follow, and more time-consuming for readers.

This prompt removes everything that doesn't improve clarity: filler phrases, lengthy explanations, softening words, and unnecessary ideas. AI is good at compression because it can see the entire meaning at once, pinpointing what is essential and what lessens impact.

The result is writing that is clear, direct, and professional—without losing nuance. This saves time for both you and your reader and reduces the back-and-forth that unclear messages often cause.

When to Use It

Use this prompt when:

- Your writing feels clunky or too long

- You need to communicate efficiently with busy people
- You're drafting something important and don't want misinterpretations
- You feel stuck editing your own work
- You need to reduce word count (emails, pitches, bios, explanations)
- You want your ideas to land cleanly the first time
- You're writing under low energy, brain fog, or time pressure

It is especially useful for:

- Emails
- Proposals
- Instructions
- Feedback
- Book paragraphs
- Public posts or announcements
- Anything going to a boss, client, or collaborator

Examples

Example 1 — Email Improvement

Input

"I wanted to follow up and see if you had a chance to look over the document I sent last week. If you haven't, no worries at all—I know how busy things can get. Just let me know whenever you have some time."

Output
"Checking in on the document I sent last week. Let me know when you've had a chance to review."

Example 2 — Overlong Explanation

Input
"The reason the project is behind is because we didn't get the materials from the vendor on time, and then the team had to reorganize the schedule. That caused further delays because we had overlapping deadlines."

Output
"The project is behind because the vendor materials arrived late, forcing us to reorganize the schedule and shifting deadlines."

Example 3 — Unclear, Rambling Text

Input
"I've been thinking about the event and maybe we should consider moving it to Saturday instead because some people said Friday might not work, though I'm not totally sure, but it could help attendance."

Output

"Consider moving the event to Saturday—several attendees said Friday doesn't work."

Variations

- Aggressive compression: "Rewrite in under 50 words."
- Minimalist version: "Rewrite using the fewest words possible without losing meaning."
- Executive version: "Rewrite for a senior leader—precise, neutral, and direct."
- Conversational: "Rewrite in a simple, casual tone but still concise."
- Technical clarity: "Rewrite for precision and logical flow."

Pro Difficulty Upgrade

Ask the model to include:

- a sentence explaining the core meaning of your original text
- a more concise rewrite + a "ultra-tight" version
- a version optimized for skimmability (bullets, headers)
- a recommended tone for the audience
- highlight what it removed and why

Example enhancement:

"Rewrite concisely, create a bullet-point version, and explain what you removed."

This turns the prompt into a clarity coaching session.

Common Mistakes to Avoid

- Accidentally removing key details when rewriting yourself
- Overexplaining simple ideas
- Adding justifications to "soften" the message
- Using long prefaces ("Just wanted to check…")
- Writing in paragraphs when a few clean sentences would work
- Letting emotion shape your word count

Clarity is kindness—especially in communication.

Template You Can Reuse
"Rewrite this so it's shorter, clearer, and easier to follow. Remove filler and redundancy. Text: [paste]."

Speed Tip
If the text is long, add: "First summarize the main point in one sentence, then rewrite the full text concisely."

This creates both a summary and an improved version.

14. Difficult Conversation Coach

Prompt
"Help me communicate a sensitive issue. Create: (1) what to say, (2) what NOT to say, (3) a calm script. Topic: [topic]."

Why It Works
Difficult conversations drain emotional and mental energy because they require you to balance honesty, clarity, empathy, and boundaries—often while managing someone else's reactions. Most people avoid these conversations or go into them unprepared, which can lead to miscommunication, escalation, or regret.

This prompt works by giving you a communication framework, not just words. It breaks the conversation into:

- What to say (the core message)
- What not to say (common pitfalls that escalate tension)
- A calm, grounded script (a ready-to-use version that preserves emotional stability)

This structure helps keep your brain regulated. Having a script reduces anxiety, prevents over-explaining, and stops reactive comments. It also makes your message clear, compassionate, and firm—no guilt spirals, no confusion, and no emotional flooding.

Over time, using this prompt develops your conflict-resolution skills and boosts your confidence in direct communication.

When to Use It

Use this prompt when:

- You need to deliver hard feedback
- You want to set a boundary
- Someone hurt or upset you
- You need to say "no" or "not right now"
- You're preparing for a tense conversation with a partner, friend, coworker, or family member
- You feel anxious or overwhelmed thinking about the conversation
- You're afraid of being misunderstood
- You want to avoid emotional escalation

It's especially powerful for:

- Performance feedback
- Family disagreements
- Money conversations
- Scheduling or workload issues
- Mismatched expectations
- Resolving miscommunication

- Relationship repairs

If you dread a conversation, this prompt gives you an anchor.

<u>Examples</u>

Example 1 — Boundaries With a Coworker

Input
Topic: A coworker keeps dumping extra tasks on you.

Output
What to say:
"I need to stick to my current workload, so I won't be able to take on additional tasks. Let's figure out a different solution."

What NOT to say:
• "I'm sorry, I know you're stressed."
• "It's fine this time, but…"
• "I guess I can try."

Calm script:
"I want to be upfront. My workload is full, so I can't take on any additional tasks. Let's look at other options to get this handled."

Example 2 — Family Conflict

Input
Topic: Someone keeps making critical comments about your parenting.

Output
What to say:
"I know you care, but the comments about my parenting feel critical. I'd prefer if you didn't give feedback unless I ask."

What NOT to say:
• "You always judge me."
• "You're being rude."
• "Whatever, I don't care."

Calm script:
"I know your intentions are good, but the comments about my parenting feel critical. I'd appreciate it if we could skip unsolicited advice. If I need input, I promise I'll ask."

Example 3 — Apology & Repair

Input
Topic: You said something hurtful and need to apologize.

Output
What to say:
"I'm sorry for what I said yesterday. I was frustrated, but that doesn't excuse it."

What NOT to say:

- "I'm sorry, but you…"
- "I only said it because…"
- "You're too sensitive."

Calm script:
"I want to apologize for what I said yesterday. It was hurtful and uncalled for. I'm taking responsibility, and I care about our relationship."

Variations

- High-stakes version: "Make the script more formal and balanced."
- Relationship version: "Make the script empathetic but clear."
- Manager version: "Make the script constructive and leadership-focused."
- Boundary-setting: "Make the script firm but not confrontational."
- Emotional regulation: "Include a one-sentence grounding reminder for me before speaking."

Pro Difficulty Upgrade

Ask the model to include:

- predicted reactions and how to respond to each
- escalation prevention tips
- clarifying questions you can use

- how to repeat your boundary if pushed
- phrases that maintain calm under pressure
- a closing line that seals the conversation

Example enhancement:

"Add predicted reactions and calm responses I can use if the conversation gets difficult."

This prepares you like a mediator or coach.

Common Mistakes to Avoid

- Apologizing excessively
- Over-explaining (weakens your boundary)
- Entering the conversation emotionally activated
- Blaming or moralizing
- Using absolutes ("you always," "you never")
- Avoiding silence—pauses are powerful
- Trying to win instead of trying to understand

A grounded tone is more effective than perfect wording.

Template You Can Reuse
"Help me communicate a sensitive issue. Include: what to say, what NOT to say, a calm script. Topic: [paste topic]."

Speed Tip
If you're highly anxious, add: "Start with one grounding sentence I can tell myself before the conversation."

It will help you regulate before speaking.

15. Presentation Prep

Prompt
"Turn this into a 5-slide outline with a hook, three key points, and a closing takeaway. [topic]"

Why It Works
Most people overprepare content and underprepare structure. The result: presentations that are dense, unfocused, and difficult to follow. This prompt reverses that. It creates a clear, concise, audience-focused outline that helps you concentrate on the core message instead of every possible detail.

Reducing your content to 5 slides—hook, three points, takeaway—effectively applies the "executive briefing" model used in high-level business settings. This format is persuasive, memorable, and simple for your audience to understand.

It also frees you from trying to design slides while you're still working through your argument. When the structure is taken care of for you, you conserve significant mental energy and cut down on preparation time. You can focus on rehearsing the storyline instead of repeatedly rewriting slides.

When to Use It

Use this prompt when:

- You need to prepare a presentation quickly
- You're unsure how to structure your talk
- Your ideas feel scattered
- You're speaking to busy people who need clarity
- You want to simplify a complex topic
- You're prepping for a pitch, internal meeting, speech, or workshop
- You feel overwhelmed staring at a blank slide deck

Especially helpful for:

- Client presentations
- Strategy updates
- Pitches and proposals
- Book talks
- Training sessions
- Executive briefings
- School or nonprofit presentations

If a presentation is stressing you out, this prompt gives you clarity and momentum.

<u>Examples</u>

Example 1 — Business Presentation

Input
Topic: Why we should expand our product into the HR market.

Output
Slide 1 — Hook:
The HR tech market is growing 11% annually, and we're missing a key opportunity.

Slides 2–4 — Three Points:

- Customer demand is shifting toward integrated solutions
- Our competitors are already entering the space
- We have a unique feature advantage that differentiates us

Slide 5 — Takeaway: Expanding into HR is our fastest path to new revenue with low risk.

Example 2 — School or Community Talk

Input
Topic: Benefits of volunteering for teens.

Output
Hook: Teens who volunteer gain the one thing school can't teach: purpose.

Three Points:

- Builds confidence
- Creates real-world skills
- Strengthens community connections

Takeaway: Volunteering isn't extra—it's foundational.

Example 3 — Author Presentation

Input
Topic: Introducing my new nonfiction book.

Output
Hook: AI won't replace you—but people who understand AI will.

Three Points:

- Why I wrote the book
- The shift happening globally
- How readers can use AI immediately

Takeaway: This book gives you a 12-month advantage in a rapidly changing world.

Variations

- Longer version: "Create a 10-slide outline with examples."
- Executive version: "Make it ultra concise with business impact up front."

- Motivational version: “Add emotional resonance to the hook and closing.”
- Data-heavy: “Suggest 3 charts or visuals to include.”
- Story-driven: “Frame the outline around a single, strong narrative arc.”

Pro Difficulty Upgrade

Ask the model to include:

- suggested visuals for each slide
- one quote or stat to elevate credibility
- pacing notes (where to pause, where to emphasize)
- potential audience objections and how to address them
- a stronger hook with an anecdote or data point
- a closing call to action customized to your audience

Example enhancement:

“Add recommended visuals and a call-to-action statement for Slide 5.”

This turns your outline into a nearly finished deck framework.

Common Mistakes to Avoid

- Cramming too much content on each slide
- Using slides as a script instead of a guide
- Starting with design instead of structure
- Forgetting to define the single takeaway you want remembered
- Overusing text instead of using visuals
- Trying to sound "smart" instead of being clear

Great presentations are simple, not dense.

Template You Can Reuse
"Create a 5-slide outline with:

- Hook
- Three key points
- Closing takeaway

Topic: [paste]."

Speed Tip: Paste any messy notes, brainstorm bullets, or a half-written outline. The model will instantly reorganize it into a clean structure, saving hours of prep.

16. Bullet-to-Paragraph Expansion

Prompt
"Turn these bullets into a smooth, well-written paragraph that flows naturally. [bullets]"

Why It Works

Thinking happens in fragments. Writing happens in flow.

Most people generate their ideas in bullet points—quick notes, scattered thoughts, fragments of meaning—but struggle to turn those bits into a polished paragraph. When you try to do it manually, your brain toggles between structuring and sentence-crafting, which dramatically increases cognitive load.

This prompt bridges the gap.

By converting bullets into a cohesive paragraph, the model does two things exceptionally well:

Creates flow
It adds transitions, connections, and ordering that human writers often miss when converting notes into narrative.

Preserves your meaning
It doesn't add fluff; it simply stitches your ideas together into a form that's ready for publication or communication.

This saves a lot of time—especially for authors, students, professionals, and anyone who outlines before drafting. Instead of struggling with sentences, you receive a clean paragraph that you can refine further if needed.

When to Use It

Use this prompt when:

- You have bullet points and need them turned into narrative
- You're drafting a book chapter, article, email, proposal, or summary
- You need to sound polished but only have fragments
- You want your writing to feel more connected and professional
- You're preparing teaching materials, blog posts, or reports
- You're suffering from brain fog and can't create flow yourself

It is especially effective for:

- Outlines
- Meeting notes
- Research summaries
- Book chapter subpoints
- Key message frameworks
- Talking points for speeches

Whenever your ideas exist in pieces, this turns them into prose.

Examples

Example 1 — Business Explanation

Input

- Customer cancellations increased
- Most occurred after onboarding
- Feedback shows confusion about setup
- We need a clearer walkthrough

Output

Customer cancellations have increased, particularly right after onboarding. Feedback suggests many customers are confused about the setup process, which means our current instructions aren't clear enough. We need to create a more straightforward walkthrough to reduce early churn.

Example 2 — Personal Writing

Input

- I miss the routine
- The kids are growing fast
- House feels different now
- Trying to adjust

Output

I miss the old routine. With the kids growing so quickly, the house feels different in ways I didn't expect, and I find myself trying to adjust to this new season of life.

Example 3 — Educational / Explanatory

Input
• Photosynthesis uses sunlight
• Plants convert CO2 and water
• Produces glucose
• Releases oxygen

Output
Photosynthesis is the process plants use to capture sunlight and convert carbon dioxide and water into glucose, which fuels their growth. In the process, they release oxygen into the atmosphere.

Variations

- Longer expansion: "Turn these bullets into two full paragraphs."
- More formal: "Create an academic-tone paragraph."
- More conversational: "Make the paragraph friendly and easy to read."
- Story-driven: "Turn these bullets into a narrative-style paragraph."
- Executive version: "Condense bullets into a tight, authoritative paragraph."

Pro Difficulty Upgrade

Ask the model to include:

- a topic sentence and concluding sentence
- improved ordering of ideas (logical sequence)

- smoother transitions between concepts
- clarity enhancements
- a parallel structure to increase readability
- a second alternative paragraph in a different tone

Example enhancement:

"Produce two paragraphs: one formal and one conversational. Add a topic sentence to each."

This helps you compare and refine your voice.

Common Mistakes to Avoid

- Listing bullets without determining the core point
- Overstuffing the paragraph with every micro-idea
- Using disjointed sentences without transitions
- Losing the thread of what the paragraph is supposed to say
- Turning outline ideas into overly detailed prose
- Forgetting that one paragraph should convey one unified idea

If the bullets cover multiple ideas, split them into two groups before expanding.

Template You Can Reuse
"Turn these bullets into a smooth, coherent paragraph with clear transitions and logical flow. Bullets: [paste]."

Speed Tip
Add: "Then give me a one-sentence summary of the paragraph."

This produces both a polished paragraph and a high-level takeaway.

17. Paragraph-to-Bullet Compression

Prompt
"Compress this text into 5–7 clean bullet points that preserve all essential ideas. Remove filler, redundancies, and side comments. Make the bullets crisp and skimmable. Text: [paste text]."

Why It Works
Humans ramble. Our natural writing process involves circling around the point, adding context, repeating key ideas, and inserting emotional framing. That's fine for drafting—but terrible for clarity. Bullets force your ideas into a clean hierarchy. They reveal structure, expose what matters, and remove everything that distracts from the core message.

This prompt converts long or messy paragraphs into precise, high-information bullet points optimized for skimming. Cognitive research shows that bullet points reduce mental load by chunking information, a method used in everything from military briefings to executive dashboards. When you express your thoughts as structured bullets, they become easier to understand, easier to act on, and easier to share.

Bullet compression is also a powerful editing tool. It shows you the skeleton of your thoughts, which helps you revise, rethink, or rewrite with radically increased clarity.

When to Use It

Use this prompt when:

- You have a long paragraph that's too dense
- You want to extract key ideas quickly
- You're preparing a summary for a busy reader
- You're refining notes into something actionable
- You're editing a chapter or article and need to see the main points
- You're converting rambling thoughts into a clean outline
- You feel overwhelmed by your own writing

This prompt is especially effective for:

- Meeting notes
- Research summaries
- Book sections
- Emails
- Reports
- Essays
- Long messages that need distillation

If someone needs the "short version," this gives it to them—and to you.

Examples

Example 1 — Work Summary

Input
"Our team missed the quarterly target because we underestimated the onboarding time for new hires and failed to adjust our schedule when two senior team members took unexpected leave. We also didn't allocate enough resources to marketing efforts."

Output
- Missed quarterly target due to longer-than-expected onboarding
- Unexpected leave from two senior members disrupted workflow
- Schedule wasn't adjusted to compensate
- Marketing efforts were under-resourced
- Combined factors slowed team output

Example 2 — Personal Reflection

Input
"I'm feeling really drained lately because the kids' schedules have been overwhelming, and I've been trying to juggle work on top of everything else. I haven't had much time for myself, and it's starting to catch up with me."

Output

- Feeling drained and overloaded
- Kids' schedules have been intense
- Work demands add pressure
- No time for personal rest
- Emotional and physical fatigue increasing

Example 3 — Informational Text

Input
"Plants grow toward light because they have cells that respond to photoreceptors. This process, called phototropism, helps them maximize sunlight absorption, which is essential for photosynthesis."

Output

- Plants grow toward light due to photoreceptors
- Process is called phototropism
- Increases sunlight absorption
- Supports photosynthesis and growth

Variations

- Ultra-tight version: “Compress into 3 bullets.”
- Extended version: “Use 10 bullets with more detail.”
- Executive summary: “Rewrite bullets for leadership-level clarity.”
- Action-oriented: “Turn the paragraph into actionable bullets.”
- Analysis version: “Add implications or risks as separate bullets.”

Pro Difficulty Upgrade

Ask the model to include:

- a one-sentence overarching summary at the top
- action items extracted from the text
- categories (e.g., causes, effects, recommendations)
- an “if you only read one bullet, read this one” bullet
- a version optimized for presentation slides
- a logic sequence (problem → cause → impact → solution)

Example enhancement:

“Compress into bullets and categorize them as problem, cause, impact, solution.”

This turns a single paragraph into a structured mental model.

Common Mistakes to Avoid

- Including too much detail per bullet
- Turning bullets into full sentences that are just paragraphs in disguise
- Adding commentary instead of extracting content
- Losing key ideas because you compressed too aggressively
- Mixing different types of information in one bullet (causes + effects)
- Forgetting that bullets should be parallel and clean

Bullets should be easy to scan, not miniature essays.

Template You Can Reuse
"Compress this into 5–7 clean bullets that preserve the core meaning. Remove filler, repetition, and anything non-essential. Text: [paste]."

Speed Tip
Add: "Then give me a second version with even tighter bullets."

This gives you two levels of compression—one for clarity, one for decision-making.

18. Executive Summary Maker

Prompt
"Summarize this into an executive brief: 150 words, plain language, key takeaways only. [paste content]"

Why It Works
Executives—and busy people in general—don't need all the details; they need the meaning of the details. They want clarity, insight, and what it all means for action. But most people summarize by simply shortening text rather than distilling it.

This prompt forces true executive thinking. Instead of restating content, it extracts:

- the core message
- the essential findings or events
- what decisions are needed
- what the implications are
- what actions follow

AI excels at this because it can analyze complex materials like notes, emails, transcripts, and lengthy documents, identifying patterns that humans might overlook. The outcome is a polished, high-level summary that resembles content prepared for a board meeting, stakeholder update, or leadership brief.

This skill saves a lot of time and cuts down on back-and-forth questions because the summary provides exactly what high-level readers need.

When to Use It

Use this prompt when:

- You need a clean, professional summary
- You're updating leadership, clients, or collaborators
- You want to turn messy notes into a coherent brief
- You have a long document that needs to be distilled quickly
- You need an overview without emotional or unnecessary detail
- You're writing for people who skim
- You're preparing your own thoughts before deciding next steps

Especially effective for:

- Project updates
- Research findings
- Meeting summaries
- Book or article analysis
- Strategic memos
- Business plans
- Performance updates

If your reader values clarity and brevity, use this.

Examples

Example 1 — Business Update

Input
Long text describing delays, staffing issues, client expectations, and budget changes.

Output
The project timeline shifted due to staffing gaps and delayed client approvals. Key priorities are reallocating resources, securing timely sign-offs, and adjusting the scope to stay within budget. Immediate next steps are aligning the revised timeline with the client and confirming internal roles for the next phase.

Example 2 — Research Summary

Input
Long paragraph explaining survey results, customer comments, and trends.

Output
Survey results show rising customer frustration with onboarding complexity. Most respondents cited unclear instructions and slow support response times. Streamlining onboarding and

improving first-week communication will address the main pain points and reduce early churn. Recommended next steps include revising the setup guide and launching a 24-hour response rule.

Example 3 — Strategic Memo

Input
Text discussing market changes, competitor actions, and product challenges.

Output
The market is shifting toward integrated solutions, and competitors have accelerated new feature releases. Our current product is strong but lacks two capabilities customers now expect. Priorities are evaluating the feasibility of fast-tracking those features and strengthening messaging around our differentiation. Recommend a focused review within one week.

Variations

- Super-short: “Rewrite as a 50-word executive snapshot.”
- Decision-only: “Highlight only what decisions need to be made.”
- Slide-ready: “Rewrite as 3–5 bullets for a presentation.”
- Action-focused: “Summarize with emphasis on next steps and responsibilities.”

- Plainest language: “Rewrite at a 7th-grade reading level but keep it executive.”

Pro Difficulty Upgrade

Ask the model to include:

- risks and opportunities
- a one-sentence top-line insight
- 3–5 next steps with owners
- what matters most to leadership
- what to watch out for over the next 30 days
- a TL;DR at the top

Example enhancement:

“Create a 150-word brief, then add a TL;DR and a risk/opportunity section.”

This transforms the summary into a high-impact strategic document.

Common Mistakes to Avoid

- Including unnecessary background context
- Thinking more detail equals more authority
- Using jargon that obscures meaning
- Overly long sentences
- Burying the lead
- Focusing on what happened instead of what matters

Executives want clarity, not density.

Template You Can Reuse
"Summarize this into a 150-word executive brief. Focus on key insights, decisions, and implications. Text: [paste]."

Speed Tip
Add: "Also give me a 1-sentence TL;DR."

This produces both a detailed executive summary and a micro-summary for fast scanning.

19. Social Posts in Your Voice

Prompt
"Create 3 social media posts in my voice using the message below. Keep each under 40 words and make them scroll-stopping, clear, and engaging. Message: [paste core message]."

Why It Works
Most people can articulate an idea, but turning that idea into a concise, high-impact social post is a completely different skill. Social platforms favor brevity, clarity, and consistent voice—and punish anything that sounds generic, corporate, or rambling.

This prompt transforms your raw idea into concise, engaging posts customized to your personal tone.

Instead of wasting time rewriting or overthinking your wording, you receive multiple polished options instantly. You can publish them right away or use them as draft inspiration.

It also encourages message discipline. Keeping posts under 40 words ensures clarity, quick reading, and emotional impact—the three key elements of content that stops scrolling. Over time, using this prompt trains your brain to communicate more precisely and effectively.

When to Use It

Use this prompt when:

- You want to post but don't know how to phrase the message
- You need short, compelling posts for Instagram, Facebook, X/Twitter, or LinkedIn
- You have a long idea that needs compressing
- You want your content to sound like you
- You're preparing for a book launch, event, or campaign
- You're batching content for the week
- You want multiple variations to test

Especially useful for:

- Announcements
- Insights
- Personal reflections
- Promotional content

- Quotes
- Educational snippets
- Calls to action

If you want clean, powerful posts without spending half an hour writing them, this prompt delivers.

Examples

Example 1 — Business Insight

Input
Message: "Small habits done consistently have a bigger impact on success than big, infrequent efforts."

Output
Success isn't built by occasional bursts—it's built by small habits repeated daily.

Big goals matter, but tiny habits decide whether we reach them.

Consistency beats intensity every time. Start small. Start today.

Example 2 — Personal Reflection

Input
Message: "I'm learning that rest is not a reward; it's part of being human."

Output
Rest isn't a prize you earn—it's fuel you need.

I'm done treating rest like a luxury. It's a requirement.

Rest is not a sign of weakness. It's a sign you're listening to your body.

Example 3 — Book Promotion

Input
Message: "My new book teaches readers how to use AI to save time and reduce stress."

Output
My new book shows you how to save hours with AI—without losing your humanity.

Ready to reclaim your time? My new AI book shows you exactly how.

AI isn't the future—it's the tool that frees your time today. The book is live.

Variations

- Add hashtags: "Include 3 relevant hashtags per post."
- Platform-specific: "Write 3 LinkedIn posts" / "Write 3 Instagram captions."

- Emotional version: “Make the posts inspiring and heartfelt.”
- Authority version: “Make the posts sound authoritative and expert.”
- Main message + call to action: “Add a CTA such as ‘learn more’ or ‘grab your copy.’”
- Carousel-friendly: “Write posts that can be broken into slide-by-slide ideas.”

Pro Difficulty Upgrade

Ask the model to include:

- three alternate tones (bold, warm, minimalist)
- platform-optimized character counts
- a version using storytelling
- a version using a question hook
- a version using a data point
- comments you can pin beneath each post
- a version you can use in a Reel or video script

Example enhancement:

“Give me 3 posts, then rewrite each in bold, warm, and minimalist tones.”

This helps you build a strong, flexible content pipeline.

Common Mistakes to Avoid

- Overexplaining the idea
- Writing posts that are too long for social attention spans
- Sounding generic or cliché
- Adding too many emojis or hashtags
- Using passive voice
- Ending the post without a hook or clear takeaway
- Posting without alignment to your actual voice

A good social post is clear, short, and emotionally resonant.

Template You Can Reuse
"Create 3 social media posts under 40 words each in my voice based on this message: [paste]."

Speed Tip
Add: "Give me 10 variations I can batch-schedule."

This turns one idea into a full week or month of content instantly.

20. Edit for Clarity & Flow

Prompt
"Edit this text for clarity, flow, and readability. Keep my voice but improve structure, tighten

wording, and smooth transitions. Note anything that weakens impact. Text: [paste text]."

Why It Works

Most writing issues aren't about ideas—they're about clarity. A paragraph can present strong points but still seem confusing if the structure is messy, transitions are weak, or the pacing is uneven. Editing your own work is tough because you're too close to it; your brain fills in gaps automatically, making it hard to see what's missing or unclear.

This prompt gives you an objective editor. The model reads your text the way a fresh reader would, identifies where meaning gets muddy, and rewrites for clarity without losing your tone. It fixes common issues like:

- sentences that run too long
- unclear references ("this," "that," "it")
- awkward phrasing
- choppy flow
- passive voice
- unnecessary repetition

Additionally, the model flags anything that weakens impact—hedging language, vague claims, filler phrases, or areas where your message loses strength. This creates writing that is clean, direct, persuasive, and easier to read.

When to Use It

Use this prompt when:

- Your writing feels clunky or "off"
- You're too close to your draft to edit effectively
- You want a more polished version of something important
- You need clean prose for a book, newsletter, email, or article
- You're editing under time pressure or brain fog
- You want a natural way to tighten your writing
- You want to maintain your voice while improving flow

Especially effective for:

- Communication with clients or leadership
- Book chapters
- Nonfiction essays
- Website copy
- Social content needing refinement
- Important emails
- Any writing that must be crystal clear

If you want your ideas to land with maximum impact, this prompt is a must.

<u>Examples</u>

Example 1 — Messy Paragraph

Input
"I wanted to reach out because things have been kind of confusing lately with the timeline, and I'm not sure if we're all on the same page. Maybe we should talk soon about what the expectations are moving forward."

Output
"I'm reaching out because the project timeline has become unclear, and I want to ensure we're aligned. Let's schedule time to clarify expectations going forward."

Example 2 — Overlong Explanation

Input
"The launch didn't go exactly how we thought it would because people weren't really prepared for the change, and some parts of the process were still unclear. We probably need to address the communication gaps."

Output
"The launch underperformed because many users weren't prepared and several process steps were unclear. We need to address the communication gaps before the next phase."

Example 3 — Book Manuscript Text

Input
"At first I didn't understand why the shift happened, but over time I realized that it wasn't about the event itself—it was about how people interpreted it and what it represented."

Output
"At first, I didn't understand the shift, but I later realized it stemmed less from the event itself and more from how people interpreted what it represented."

Variations

- More formal: "Edit for academic tone."
- More conversational: "Edit to sound natural and friendly."
- More authoritative: "Strengthen voice and remove hedging."
- More concise: "Cut 20% of the words without losing meaning."
- More emotional: "Increase warmth and empathy while staying clear."
- More punch: "Make the writing sharper and more impactful."

Pro Difficulty Upgrade

Ask the model to include:

- a line-by-line explanation of the changes

- a highlighted version showing edits
- suggestions to further improve logic or structure
- questions that reveal unclear areas
- alternate versions (shorter, more formal, more narrative)
- a readability score and how to improve it
- potential layout changes for formatting (bullets, headings, breaks)

Example enhancement:

"Edit for clarity, then show me a tracked-changes style version."

This teaches you how and why the edit works.

Common Mistakes to Avoid

- Editing while emotionally attached to your original wording
- Adding more words instead of clarifying
- Leaving sentences where the subject or object is unclear
- Using vague language ("some people," "things," "stuff")
- Ignoring rhythm—good writing flows like speech
- Thinking clarity diminishes artistry (it strengthens it)

Clear writing is not simple writing—it's deliberate writing.

Template You Can Reuse
"Edit this text for clarity, structure, and flow. Keep my voice, but tighten and smooth. Text: [paste]."

Speed Tip
If you want deeper refinement, add:

"Also provide a 2-sentence summary of what you think I'm trying to say."

This confirms whether the text communicates your intended meaning.

Chapter 4 — Work & Career (10 Prompts)

Work involves decision-making, prioritization, communication, and strategy—yet most people spend their days reacting rather than leading. The prompts in this section are designed to give you professional leverage: clearer choices, stronger thinking, faster execution, and more efficient workflows.

Whether you're an employee, manager, freelancer, business owner, or creator, these prompts will help you operate like someone with a chief of staff—focused, strategic, and proactive about problems instead of always responding to them.

21. Strategy Simulator

Prompt
"Help me think strategically. Based on this goal: [paste goal], generate (1) strategic options, (2) one recommended approach, and (3) the first three steps to move forward."

Why It Works
Many people confuse tasks with strategy. When you are too close to your work, you tend to focus only on what needs to be done next, not on which direction to take or why. Strategy involves

evaluating options, trade-offs, and selecting the path that offers the highest return on time and effort. However, doing this alone is challenging because the brain naturally defaults to what feels familiar.

This prompt encourages a strategic pause. By generating multiple options, it broadens your perspective. Instead of settling on the first idea that comes up, you can explore alternative paths that might have higher rewards or lower risks. The model also objectively assesses the options, providing you with a recommended approach free from emotional bias.

Finally, it bridges the gap from strategy to tactics by providing you with the first three steps. This is essential. Ideas are worthless without action. Those three steps give you progress, clarity, and momentum.

When to Use It

Use this prompt when:

- You're starting a new project
- You're choosing between multiple paths
- You want clarity before committing resources
- You feel stuck and don't know what direction to take

- You want to think like an executive, not an operator
- You need to present options to leadership or clients
- You're planning a pivot, launch, or major decision
- You want to ensure your actions align with your long-term goals

Especially powerful for:

- Business growth planning
- Career decisions
- Creative direction for books or content
- Project roadmapping
- Financial or operational decisions
- Marketing strategy

If you feel overwhelmed or directionless, this prompt will anchor you.

<u>Examples</u>

Example 1 — Business Goal

Input
Goal: Grow my consulting business over the next six months.

Output
Strategic Options:

- Specialize in a niche and raise prices

- Launch a small-group coaching program
- Partner with complementary businesses

Recommended Approach:
Niche specialization + targeted partnerships for credibility and referrals.

First Three Steps:

- Identify niche (based on past profitable clients)
- Update messaging and website
- Reach out to 5 partnership candidates

Example 2 — Career Goal

Input
Goal: Move into a leadership role at my company.

Output
Strategic Options:

- Position yourself as the owner of cross-departmental initiatives
- Mentor junior teammates
- Present improvement recommendations to leadership

Recommended Approach: Lead a high-impact initiative that fills a gap leadership hasn't fully solved.

First Three Steps:

- Identify high-friction area in the company
- Draft a 30-day improvement plan
- Present it to manager for alignment

Example 3 — Creative Goal

Input
Goal: Increase visibility for my book launch.

Output
Strategic Options:

- Build a 30-day content campaign
- Run targeted ads
- Partner with podcasters and influencers

Recommended Approach: Start with partnerships: fastest reach, highest trust.

First Three Steps:

- Build a list of 30 aligned podcasts
- Create 3 pitch templates
- Send 10 pitches per week

Variations

- Risk-sensitive version: “Include risks and mitigation strategies for each option.”
- Data-driven: “Include metrics to measure success for each strategy.”
- Creative industry: “Generate bold, unconventional strategies too.”

- Leadership version: "Add implications for team, budget, and timeline."
- Investor version: "Add ROI potential and resource requirements."

Pro Difficulty Upgrade

Ask the model to include:

- a SWOT analysis
- time horizon (short-term vs. long-term strategy)
- a "minimum viable strategy" if resources are low
- second-order consequences (what this choice leads to next)
- an anti-goal (what you want to avoid)
- how competitors would approach the same goal
- scenario analysis (best, mid, worst case)

Example enhancement:

"Add SWOT, risk analysis, and a minimum-viable path I could start this week."

This elevates you into true strategic thinking.

Common Mistakes to Avoid

- Jumping into tactics without exploring options

- Choosing the most familiar path instead of the best one
- Trying to pursue multiple strategies at once
- Overcomplicating the plan
- Ignoring resource and time constraints
- Underestimating activation energy required

Strategy is choosing—and choosing means not choosing everything.

Template You Can Reuse
"Help me think strategically. For my goal [paste], give me:

- Strategic options
- One recommended approach
- First three steps."

Speed Tip
Add: "Then rewrite the recommendation as a pitch I can use with stakeholders."

This turns your strategy into a communication-ready proposal.

22. Pros/Cons Analyzer

Prompt
"Provide a pros/cons analysis for the following decision. Then give me the 'If nothing changes…' scenario to clarify the cost of inaction. Decision: [paste decision]."

Why It Works
Most people evaluate decisions by instinct rather than structure. They mentally switch between options, consider hypothetical outcomes, and get caught in emotional loops. However, effective decision-making needs a clear comparison of benefits, risks, and consequences. The pros/cons list remains timeless because it presents information in a simple, comparable way.

This prompt enhances the traditional approach by including something most people overlook: the cost of doing nothing. Humans naturally fear making the wrong decision, but they rarely think about the dangers of inaction. This leads to stagnation. By highlighting what occurs if the current situation stays the same, AI helps overcome decision paralysis and reveals the true stakes.

Finally, the analysis remains neutral and free of emotion. The model isn't influenced by fear, ego, fatigue, guilt, or optimism. It provides a clear, objective view of your options—often revealing the best path with surprising clarity.

When to Use It

Use this prompt when:

- You're stuck between two or more choices

- You're procrastinating on a meaningful decision
- Emotions are clouding your thinking
- You need clarity fast
- You're weighing financial, career, or relationship options
- You want a neutral breakdown without bias
- You're preparing to justify a decision to someone else

Especially effective for:

- Career moves
- Business investments
- Creative directions
- Household purchases
- Whether to start, pause, or end a project
- Time commitment decisions (e.g., volunteering, social obligations)

If you hate making decisions, this prompt stabilizes the process.

<u>Examples</u>

Example 1 — Should You Start a Freelance Business?

Input
Decision: Start a freelance consulting business on the side.

Output
Pros:

- Additional income
- Build portfolio
- Gain autonomy
- Test new skills without leaving job

Cons:

- Time commitment
- Income inconsistency
- Steeper learning curve

If nothing changes: You stay dependent on your primary income and miss a low-risk window to build something new.

Example 2 — Should You Move Cities?

Input
Decision: Move to a different city for a job.

Output
Pros:
• Higher salary
• Better career opportunities
• Fresh environment

Cons:
• Relocation stress
• Social reset
• Higher cost of living

If nothing changes: Career growth remains slow, and similar opportunities may not appear again soon.

Example 3 — Should You Outsource a Task?

Input
Decision: Hire someone to manage your social media.

Output
Pros:

- Saves 5+ hours/week
- More consistent posting
- Professional-quality content

Cons:

- Cost
- Requires onboarding
- Less personal control

If nothing changes: You continue losing hours to a task that isn't your highest-leverage work.

Variations

- Two-option comparison: "Compare Option A vs. B side-by-side."
- Multi-option: "Include three or more alternatives."

- Risk-first version: “Highlight risks first, then benefits.”
- Emotional impact: “Include emotional pros/cons too.”
- Long-term angle: “List only long-term pros/cons (5–10 years).”

Pro Difficulty Upgrade

Ask the model to include:

- weighted scoring (importance 1–10)
- decision criteria (cost, time, impact, risk)
- a recommended choice based on your goals
- potential unintended consequences
- what the decision looks like in best/mid/worst-case scenarios
- questions you should ask before deciding
- the 30-day, 90-day, and 1-year impacts

Example enhancement:

“Add a weighted scoring matrix and a recommended decision based on minimizing future regret.”

This upgrades you into a structured decision-maker.

Common Mistakes to Avoid

- Overemphasizing short-term discomfort

- Ignoring long-term consequences
- Waiting for absolute certainty (it never comes)
- Confusing fear with intuition
- Overvaluing sunk costs
- Treating pros/cons as equally important

A decision is rarely about quantity of pros—it's about quality.

Template You Can Reuse
"Provide a pros/cons analysis for this decision. Then give the 'If nothing changes…' scenario. Decision: [paste]."

Speed Tip
If you're spinning, add: "Now tell me the smallest next step that moves me closer to a decision."

This breaks paralysis instantly.

23. Market Research Short Report

Prompt
"Create a short market research report with: (1) key trends, (2) customer insights, (3) competitor snapshot, and (4) opportunities. Topic/industry: [paste topic]. Keep it clear, skimmable, and insight-driven."

Why It Works

Traditional market research is slow, tedious, and often overwhelming. It involves sorting through trends, customer pain points, competitor offerings, pricing, messaging, and gaps—all of which can take hours. Most people give up before gaining clarity.

This prompt condenses that process into a high-level, insight-rich report that gives you the essentials fast:

- Trends — Where the market is shifting
- Customer insights — What buyers care about
- Competitor snapshot — Who's doing what
- Opportunities — Where you can win

The model links patterns across industries, customer behavior, and competitive strategy. Instead of getting overwhelmed by data, you receive the refined insights that truly matter for decision-making.

Whether you're launching a product, writing a book, starting a business, or exploring a niche, this report gives you a sharp strategic overview in minutes.

When to Use It

Use this prompt when:

- You're testing a business idea

- You want to know if a niche is profitable
- You're preparing a pitch or proposal
- You're refining your value proposition
- You need to understand audience needs
- You want a quick assessment before deeper research
- You're comparing multiple project ideas
- You want to avoid pursuing a dead-end market

Especially helpful for:

- Authors researching book niches
- Entrepreneurs assessing markets
- Creators validating content ideas
- Freelancers exploring service lines
- Product teams defining features

This prompt helps you make smart, informed, opportunity-driven decisions.

Examples

Example 1 — Fitness App Market

Input
Topic: A mobile app for at-home strength training.

Output
Key Trends:

- Rise in hybrid home/ gym workouts
- Demand for simple, personalized plans

- Preference for quick sessions (10–20 min)

Customer Insights:

- Overwhelmed by complex programs
- Want visible progress and accountability
- Need workouts that fit unpredictable schedules

Competitor Snapshot:

- Big apps focus on high intensity or premium coaching
- Few offer beginner-friendly strength guidance
- Most lack true personalization

Opportunities:

- Create simple, progressive strength paths
- Build in micro-workouts
- Offer adaptive programming for busy lifestyles

Example 2 — Parenting Book Market

Input
Topic: A book on raising emotionally intelligent kids.

Output
Key Trends:

- Strong interest in emotional regulation

- Growth in trauma-informed parenting content
- Parents seeking scripts and real examples

Customer Insights:

- Feel overwhelmed by theory-heavy books
- Want practical tools
- Prefer short, actionable sections

Competitor Snapshot:

- Many bestsellers focus on discipline
- Fewer focus on emotional literacy
- Some are overly academic for general audiences

Opportunities:

- Provide real-life scripts
- Highlight quick exercises
- Target busy parents with modular chapters

Example 3 — Pet Product Market

Input
Topic: Premium cat enrichment toys.

Output
Key Trends:

- Growth in enrichment products
- Human-grade materials trending
- Customers value durability and mental stimulation

Customer Insights:

- Want toys that last
- Seek products that reduce boredom
- Prefer enrichment over cheap novelty toys
- Competitor Snapshot:
- Many brands are low-quality plastic
- High-end options expensive but limited
- Few offer species-specific enrichment

Opportunities:

- Launch durable, natural-material toys
- Offer enrichment guides
- Create targeted toys (indoor-only cats, high-energy cats, seniors)

Variations

- Deep-dive: “Expand each section to 3–5 bullets.”
- Quantitative version: “Add rough demand estimates or market size.”
- Pricing insights: “Include competitor pricing ranges and customer price sensitivity.”
- Positioning focus: “Add messaging gaps competitors aren’t addressing.”
- Creative industry: “Add genre trends and audience psychographics.”
- B2B: “Add buying triggers and decision-maker types.”

Pro Difficulty Upgrade

Ask the model to include:

- what's declining or becoming outdated
- hidden opportunities competitors ignore
- underserved segments
- underserved content niches (for authors/creators)
- early indicators of future trends
- three market-entry angles
- one "wild card" disruptive angle

Example enhancement:

"Add an underserved audience segment and three angles for entering the market."

This transforms your research into a strategic blueprint.

Common Mistakes to Avoid

- Mistaking trends for opportunities
- Overvaluing saturated markets
- Ignoring customer pain points
- Focusing too much on competitors instead of gaps
- Copying what others do instead of differentiating
- Skipping customer insights entirely

Market research is only useful if it leads to action—and opportunity.

Template You Can Reuse

"Create a short market research report with:

- Key trends
- Customer insights
- Competitor snapshot
- Opportunities

Topic: [paste]."

Speed Tip

Add: "Then give me the one biggest opportunity in a single sentence."

The model will surface the clearest, highest-value path forward.

24. Policy Explainer

Prompt

"Explain this policy in simple, practical terms. Include: (1) what it means, (2) why it exists, (3) how it affects me, and (4) one example of real-world impact. Policy: [paste policy]."

Why It Works

Policies—whether corporate, legal, governmental, or procedural—are written for compliance, not comprehension. They are often dense, jargon-filled, and full of abstract language that hides the real-world meaning. When you try to understand a policy, your brain wastes energy translating legalese into useful information.

This prompt cuts through the complexity by breaking the policy into four essential components:

1. What it means — plain-language translation
2. Why it exists — the purpose or rationale
3. How it affects you — the practical implications for your daily life or work
4. Real-world example — concrete clarity through scenario

This structure mirrors how regulatory experts, lawyers, and compliance officers think—but without the jargon. It gives you a precise, accessible understanding so you can make decisions confidently and avoid misunderstandings.

When to Use It

Use this prompt when:

- You're reading a dense corporate or HR policy
- You need to understand changes to company rules
- You're reviewing legal, insurance, or financial documents

- You're analyzing government policies and regulations
- You want to explain a policy to a team or client
- You're preparing training or onboarding materials
- You need to understand exactly what's allowed or required

Especially useful for:

- HR policies
- PTO, benefits, and leave rules
- Safety and compliance policies
- Data privacy and security rules
- Insurance terms
- School or community policies
- Public laws
- New procedures at work

If something feels confusing or you want total clarity, this prompt delivers it.

Examples

Example 1 — Workplace Remote Work Policy

Input
Policy: "Employees may work remotely up to two days per week with manager approval. Exceptions require HR review."

Output
What it means: You can work from home two days a week, but only if your manager signs off.

Why it exists: The company wants flexibility while ensuring teams stay coordinated.

How it affects you: You need to plan your remote days in advance and communicate with your manager.

Real-world example: If you want to work from home three days next week, you'll need a specific exception through HR.

Example 2 — Insurance Policy Clause

Input
Policy: "Pre-existing conditions are not covered for the first 12 months."

Output
What it means: If you had a medical condition before your coverage started, the plan won't pay for related treatment for the first year.

Why it exists: Insurance companies limit early claims from conditions they didn't price into your policy.

How it affects you: You may need to pay out-of-pocket for treatment until month 13.

Real-world example: If you had asthma before enrolling, inhaler refills and appointments won't be covered for the first year.

Example 3 — Data Privacy Policy

Input
Policy: "We may share anonymized user data for analytical purposes."

Output
What it means: Your data may be used for research, but identifying details are removed.

Why it exists: Companies use data to understand users and improve products.

How it affects you: Your usage patterns may be analyzed, but you won't be personally identifiable.

Real-world example: Your click behavior may inform how a website redesigns its navigation menu.

Variations

- Extended version: "Include risks, exceptions, and who to contact with questions."

- For training: “Rewrite for clarity and then create a 3-bullet teaching version.”
- For leadership: “Include how this policy affects team management.”
- For customers: “Rewrite as customer-friendly guidance.”
- Legal tone: “Preserve precision while simplifying language.”
- Family version: “Rewrite at a 6th-grade reading level.”

Pro Difficulty Upgrade

Ask the model to include:

- a condensed 30-second explanation you can use verbally
- a table of “allowed vs. not allowed” scenarios
- interpretations of edge cases
- who benefits and who loses from the policy
- potential unintended consequences
- questions you should ask HR/Legal
- a checklist of what you must do to comply

Example enhancement:
“Add a 30-second elevator explanation and a list of questions I should ask before signing anything.”

This makes your policy understanding actionable and complete.

Common Mistakes to Avoid

- Assuming policies are intuitive—they rarely are
- Ignoring exceptions or fine print
- Misinterpreting vague language
- Thinking policy equals suggestion (it's binding)
- Believing "manager discretion" always works in your favor
- Overlooking real-world consequences for non-compliance

Clarity protects you—professionally and legally.

Template You Can Reuse
"Explain this policy in simple terms with:
what it means, why it exists, how it affects me and give me a real-world example, here is the policy: [paste]."

Speed Tip
Add: "Also list any red flags or areas where misinterpretation is common."

This gives you both clarity and caution in one pass.

25. Sales Page Draft

Prompt

"Turn this offer into a persuasive sales page with: (1) a strong hook, (2) who it's for, (3) the core promise, (4) key benefits, and (5) a clear call to action. Keep it simple, compelling, and skimmable. Offer: [paste details]."

Why It Works
A sales page is not about hype—it's about clarity. Most people struggle with sales writing because they either:

- oversell (making it sound exaggerated),
- undersell (making it sound vague), or
- confuse features with benefits.

This prompt solves those problems instantly by forcing a proven structure used in high-converting sales pages:

- Hook — grabs attention
- Audience — makes the reader feel seen
- Promise — the transformation or result
- Benefits — what life looks like if they say yes

Call to Action (CTA) = what to do next

This removes guesswork and makes your page persuasive without sounding "salesy." The model converts your idea into a message that appeals both emotionally and logically, while remaining consistent with your tone.

Because the structure is universal, you can reuse it for books, services, courses, digital products, coaching, apps, or events.

When to Use It

Use this prompt when:

- You're launching a new product or service
- You want a simple, convincing book landing page
- You're creating a Kickstarter, Indiegogo, or pre-order page
- You're building an Amazon listing description
- You need a website sales section
- You're writing a pitch page for clients or employers
- You're testing different angles to see what resonates
- You're stuck staring at a blank page

It's especially effective when writing for:

- Book promotion
- Online courses
- Coaching programs
- Software tools
- Freelance services
- Workshops or events
- Digital downloads
- Membership communities

A powerful sales page can double or triple conversions. This prompt helps you achieve that quickly.

Examples

Example 1 — Book Sales Page

Input
Offer: A book that teaches parents emotional coaching skills.

Output
Hook: What if the most powerful parenting tool isn't discipline—it's emotional literacy?

Who It's For: Parents who want calmer homes, stronger communication, and kids who feel understood.

Core Promise: Teach your child to identify, express, and manage emotions with confidence.

Key Benefits:

- Fewer meltdowns
- More cooperation
- Stronger parent–child trust
- Scripts and tools you can use today

CTA: Get the book and transform your family dynamics.

Example 2 — Service Offering

Input
Offer: Monthly bookkeeping for small businesses.

Output
Hook: Stop drowning in receipts. Start focusing on your business.

Who It's For: Small business owners who want clean books without spending hours doing it themselves.

Core Promise: Accurate, stress-free financials every month.

Key Benefits:

- Know your numbers at a glance
- Avoid tax-time panic
- Make smarter decisions
- Reclaim 5–10 hours per month

CTA: Book your free consultation.

Example 3 — Digital Product

Input
Offer: A Notion template for content planning.

Output

Hook: Create content consistently—even when you're overwhelmed.

Who It's For: Creators, entrepreneurs, and marketers.

Core Promise: A plug-and-play content system that keeps you organized and ahead.

Key Benefits:

- Weekly content planning
- Simple idea tracker
- Built-in analytics
- Never stare at a blank page again

CTA: Download the template instantly.

Variations

- Short-form: "Write a compact sales blurb under 120 words."
- Long-form: "Expand into a full 1,000-word sales page with sections."
- Brand voice: "Rewrite in a warm/authoritative/minimalist voice."
- Feature-heavy: "Add a detailed feature breakdown."
- Emotion-first: "Lead with emotional benefits rather than features."
- Problem–Solution: "Rewrite in problem → agitation → solution format."

- Amazon-ready: "Format for an Amazon book description."
- Workshop version: "Add urgency and limited availability."

Pro Difficulty Upgrade

Ask the model to include:

- three alternate hooks
- objections + responses
- a comparison table (you vs. alternatives)
- social proof placeholders
- reader/customer transformation statements
- a final CTA written in three styles
- two optional angles (emotional and practical)

Example enhancement:

"Rewrite with objections, a comparison table, and three alternate hooks."

This turns your sales page into conversion-focused copy.

Common Mistakes to Avoid

- Focusing on features instead of outcomes
- Sounding robotic, vague, or overly hype-heavy
- Writing too much (readers skim sales pages)

- Writing too little (readers need clarity)
- Leaving out the "who it's for" section
- Forgetting to tell people what to do next
- Assuming benefits are obvious—they aren't
- Not using a hook that grabs attention in 3 seconds

Your sales page should make the reader think: "This is exactly for me."

Template You Can Reuse
"Turn this offer into a persuasive sales page with:

- Hook
- Who it's for
- Core promise
- Key benefits
- CTA

Offer: [paste]."

Speed Tip
Add: "Now give me a second version in a totally different angle."

This lets you A/B test instantly.

26. Grant or Pitch Draft

Prompt
"Turn this idea into a compelling pitch/grant narrative. Include: (1) the problem, (2) why it matters, (3) your proposed solution, (4) expected

impact, and (5) what you need from the reader/funder. Idea: [paste idea]."

Why It Works
Grants and pitches fail for one of three reasons:

- The problem isn't clearly defined
- The solution doesn't feel credible or specific
- The impact isn't articulated in tangible terms

Most proposals get lost in jargon or vague language, causing funders or stakeholders to tune out. They seek clarity, purpose, and proof that their money or approval will lead to real change.

This prompt uses a 5-part narrative framework that reflects how successful grants and pitches are organized.

- The problem — urgent and clearly framed
- Why it matters — stakes and context
- Your solution — specific, actionable, credible
- Impact — measurable outcomes, not vague claims
- Ask — what you need from the reader

This turns your idea into a persuasive, high-trust narrative that funders, stakeholders, or decision-makers can quickly understand and support.

When to Use It

Use this prompt when:

- Writing a grant application
- Pitching a business idea
- Proposing a project to leadership
- Applying for funding, partnerships, or sponsorships
- Presenting an initiative to a board or committee
- Crafting a pitch deck narrative
- Preparing for a live pitch or presentation
- Writing a query letter for a nonfiction book

It is especially useful for:

- Nonprofits
- Startups
- Creative projects
- Research proposals
- Author or book pitches
- Educational programs
- Community initiatives

If you need buy-in, support, funding, or approval, this prompt gives you the structure.

<u>Examples</u>

Example 1 — Nonprofit Grant

Input
Idea: After-school STEM program for underserved youth.

Output
Problem: Many underserved students lack access to after-school STEM opportunities, widening the achievement gap.

Why it matters: Without intervention, these students enter high school and college unprepared for careers in a rapidly changing technical economy.

Solution: A free, after-school STEM program staffed by trained mentors offering weekly hands-on sessions.

Impact: Students gain confidence, skills, and early exposure to tech careers. We anticipate a 30% increase in STEM course participation.

The Ask: We request $25,000 to fund materials, mentor training, and curriculum development.

Example 2 — Business Pitch

Input

Idea: A meal-planning app for busy professionals.

Output
Problem: Busy professionals waste time planning meals and often resort to unhealthy last-minute choices.

Why it matters: Poor diet and decision fatigue reduce productivity, energy, and long-term health.

Solution: An AI-powered app that generates weekly meal plans, grocery lists, and quick recipes tailored to user preferences.

Impact: Users save 3–5 hours a week and improve nutrition consistency.

The Ask: Seeking $150K to complete development and launch a beta program.

Example 3 — Book Pitch

Input
Idea: A nonfiction book about how small habits transform long-term identity.

Output
Problem: People chase big transformation but fail because habits are inconsistent or misaligned with identity.

Why it matters: The self-improvement industry overwhelms readers with advice that doesn't stick.

Solution: A practical guide showing how micro-habits reshape identity through a 4-step, research-backed framework.

Impact: Readers build sustainable habits and experience lasting personal growth.

The Ask: Seeking agent/publisher partnership to bring this book to market.

Variations

- Slide-ready: "Rewrite this as a 5-slide pitch deck narrative."
- Investor-focused: "Add ROI and projected outcomes."
- Grant-specific: "Align with typical grant language: need, approach, outcomes."
- Scientific: "Add research justification and methodology."
- Community-oriented: "Add community testimonials or proposed partnerships."
- Nonprofit version: "Add equity, inclusion, and access components."

Pro Difficulty Upgrade

Ask the model to include:

- measurable success metrics

- risks and mitigation strategies
- 1–2 quotes or testimonials (can be placeholders)
- sustainability plan (how the project continues long term)
- budget summary
- timeline with milestones
- emotional resonance (story or anecdote)

Example enhancement:

"Add impact metrics, a timeline, and a short anecdote to strengthen emotional appeal."

This turns your pitch into a full funding-ready narrative.

Common Mistakes to Avoid

- Using abstract language or jargon without concrete details or explanation
- Overexplaining the solution before defining the problem
- Leaving out measurable outcomes
- Not explaining why this matters now
- Forgetting to specify what you're asking for
- Writing too academically or with too much jargon
- Making the proposal about you instead of the problem

A pitch is a story about transformation—your idea is the catalyst.

Template You Can Reuse
"Turn this idea into a pitch with:

- The problem
- Why it matters
- The solution
- Expected impact
- The ask

Idea: [paste]."

Speed Tip
If your idea isn't fully formed yet, write: "Help me articulate the idea clearly first."

The model will clean your concept before turning it into a pitch.

27. Process Mapping

Prompt
"Turn this workflow into a clear, step-by-step process map. Include: (1) stages, (2) actions, (3) who is responsible, and (4) handoffs. Make it simple and visual. Workflow: [paste workflow]."

Why It Works
Most work problems, including bottlenecks, delays, and confusion, arise from one main issue: no one truly understands the actual process.

Teams assume they share the same understanding, but in reality:

- steps get skipped
- responsibilities overlap
- people duplicate work
- no one knows when a task is "done enough"
- handoffs are unclear

As a result, projects bog down and people blame each other rather than the process.

This prompt produces a clear process map that emphasizes sequence, ownership, and handoffs—the three pillars of operational efficiency. It follows the same method used by operations consultants and lean specialists to simplify systems.

The magic lies in its simplicity. Instead of a cluttered, overly complicated diagram, you get a straightforward map you can easily use, share, or improve.

When to Use It

Use this prompt when:

- A workflow feels chaotic or unclear
- You're onboarding someone
- You're delegating a recurring task
- A project keeps getting stuck

- You want more consistency across a team
- You're documenting SOPs
- You want to reduce errors or rework
- You need to prepare a clean explanation for leadership or clients

Especially powerful for:

- Content creation workflows
- Customer onboarding
- Sales pipelines
- Publishing processes
- Hiring processes
- Bookkeeping
- Book production
- Product development
- Event planning

If something happens more than twice, it needs a map.

<u>Examples</u>

Example 1 — Content Creation Workflow

Input
Workflow: blog from idea → draft → edit → publish → promote

Output
Stage 1: Ideation

- Action: Generate topics

- Owner: You
- Handoff: Send selected idea to writer

Stage 2: Drafting
- Action: Writer produces draft
- Owner: Writer
- Handoff: Return draft to editor

Stage 3: Editing
- Action: Edit for clarity and structure
- Owner: Editor
- Handoff: Send final to publisher

Stage 4: Publishing
- Action: Upload, format, publish
- Owner: Publisher
- Handoff: Notify marketing

Stage 5: Promotion
- Action: Social posts + email newsletter
- Owner: Marketing
- Handoff: None

Example 2 — Hiring Process

Input
Workflow: job posted → applications reviewed → interviews → offer → onboarding

Output
Stage 1: Posting

- Action: Write and publish job description
- Owner: Hiring Manager
- Handoff: Recruiter

Stage 2: Screening

- Action: Review resumes + phone screen
- Owner: Recruiter
- Handoff: Hiring Manager

Stage 3: Interviews

- Action: Conduct interviews + score candidates
- Owner: Hiring Panel
- Handoff: Hiring Manager

Stage 4: Offer

- Action: Draft offer + negotiate
- Owner: HR
- Handoff: Payroll

Stage 5: Onboarding

- Action: Setup accounts, training, orientation
- Owner: HR
- Handoff: Team Lead

Example 3 — Book Publishing (Independent Author)

Input
Workflow: manuscript → edit → design → publish → launch

Output

Stage 1: Manuscript Completion

- Action: Finish draft
- Owner: Author
- Handoff: Editor

Stage 2: Editing

- Action: Developmental + line edits
- Owner: Editor
- Handoff: Author for revisions

Stage 3: Design

- Action: Format interior + design cover
- Owner: Designer
- Handoff: Publisher/KDP

Stage 4: Publishing

- Action: Upload to KDP/IS, review proof
- Owner: Author
- Handoff: Marketing

Stage 5: Launch

- Action: Announce, run ads, send newsletter
- Owner: Author/Marketing
- Handoff: Ongoing promotion

Variations

- Visual version: "Format as a vertical flowchart."

- Simplified version: "Summarize into five stages only."
- Detailed: "Add tools or software to use at each step."
- Delegation-focused: "Emphasize who does what and what they need."
- Efficiency version: "Identify bottlenecks and quick improvements."
- Automation version: "Highlight steps that can be automated with AI."

Pro Difficulty Upgrade

Ask the model to include:

- failure points (where work typically breaks down)
- improvements with high ROI
- estimated time per step
- dependency mapping
- a checklist for each stage
- best practices
- indicators that something is going off track
- one "make this faster" recommendation

Example enhancement:

"Map the process and include bottlenecks, quick wins, and automation opportunities."

This transforms your workflow from reactive to optimized.

Common Mistakes to Avoid

- Assuming everyone knows the process—often they don't
- Mixing tasks that should be sequential
- Forgetting to define handoffs
- Leaving ownership vague ("team," "we," "marketing")
- Including too much detail (makes maps unusable)
- Using jargon instead of simple language

A process map works best when it's simple, clear, and followed.

Template You Can Reuse

"Turn this workflow into a clear process map with:

- Stages
- Actions
- Owners
- Handoffs
- Workflow: [paste]."

Speed Tip

Add: "Now create a one-page SOP from this map."

The model will convert the process map into a standardized operating procedure.

28. SOP Generator

Prompt
"Create a clear, step-by-step Standard Operating Procedure (SOP) using this workflow. Include: (1) purpose, (2) scope, (3) responsibilities, (4) detailed steps, and (5) quality checks. Workflow: [paste workflow]."

Why It Works
An SOP is the backbone of consistent, repeatable work. Without one, tasks rely on memory, interpretation, and individual habits—which leads to:

- inconsistent results
- onboarding problems
- mistakes and rework
- communication gaps
- inefficiency and frustration

Most people avoid creating SOPs because writing them feels tedious and complicated. This prompt handles the structure for you. It transforms your workflow into a professional-grade SOP that defines what the task is, who does it, how it's done, and how to ensure it's done correctly.

The result is clarity: anyone can follow the procedure—even months later—and produce consistent outcomes.

When to Use It

Use this prompt when:

- You're delegating work
- You need consistency across a team
- A task is repeated weekly, monthly, or seasonally
- You want clearer operations in your business
- You're creating documentation for hiring or outsourcing
- You want to reduce mistakes or quality issues
- You're preparing for scaling or growth
- You need a reference document you can hand off anytime

Especially powerful for:

- Social media workflows
- Book publishing processes
- Client onboarding
- Customer support
- Marketing campaigns
- Administrative routines
- Bookkeeping
- Event planning
- Household management (yes—this works at home too)

If you repeat it more than twice, it should have an SOP.

<u>Examples</u>

Example 1 — Monthly Newsletter SOP

Input
Workflow: draft → edit → design → schedule → send → track metrics

Output
Purpose: Ensure consistent, high-quality monthly newsletters.

Scope: Applies to all email campaigns sent to subscribers.

Responsibilities:

- Writer: drafts content
- Editor: reviews and edits
- Designer: formats in template
- Marketing: schedules and tracks metrics

Steps:

1. Draft newsletter using monthly content plan
2. Editor reviews for clarity and accuracy
3. Designer formats with brand template
4. Marketing schedules send date/time
5. After sending, marketing records open/click rates within 48 hours
6. Quality Checks:
    - All links tested
    - Tone consistent with brand
    - Mobile formatting verified

Example 2 — Client Onboarding SOP

Input
Workflow: intake form → kickoff call → contract → payment → project start

Output
Purpose: Create a smooth onboarding experience for new clients.

Scope: All new service-based client engagements.

Responsibilities:

- Client Coordinator: collects forms and schedules call
- Project Manager: leads kickoff and prepares scope
- Finance: handles payment and contracts

Steps:

1. Send intake form and welcome email
2. Client completes form
3. Coordinator schedules kickoff call
4. Project Manager reviews form, prepares agenda
5. Kickoff call held
6. Contract sent after alignment
7. Payment processed
8. Project officially begins
9. Quality Checks:
    - Contract matches scope discussed

- Payment confirmed before work
- Client has all onboarding materials

Example 3 — Book Publishing SOP

Input
Workflow: final draft → edit → format → upload → proof → publish

Output
Purpose: Ensure a clean, error-free book publishing workflow.

Scope: Covers all self-published titles (paperback, hardcover, ebook).

Responsibilities:

- Author: final draft
- Editor: edits
- Designer: formatting + cover
- Publisher: uploads, proofs, approves

Steps:

1. Finalize manuscript
2. Send to editor for developmental + line edits
3. Revise based on feedback
4. Designer formats interior + cover
5. files to KDP/IS
6. Order proof copy
7. Review proof + fix issues

8. Approve for publication
9. Quality Checks:
    - No widows/orphans
    - Cover meets sizing requirements
    - Proof copy read fully before approval

Variations

- Blueprint version: "Add tools, templates, and scripts for each step."
- Delegation-friendly: "Write SOP for someone with no prior experience."
- Lean version: "Highlight wasteful steps and propose streamlining."
- AI-automation: "Identify which steps can be automated with AI."
- Client presentation: "Rewrite SOP in clean, client-facing language."
- Checklist version: "Add a checklist at the end for quick review."

Pro Difficulty Upgrade

Ask the model to include:

- time estimates per step
- dependencies and prerequisites
- risks + mitigation
- common errors and how to avoid them
- templates for emails or scripts
- a RACI chart (Responsible, Accountable, Consulted, Informed)

- version control notes
- KPI suggestions (how to measure success)

Example enhancement:

"Add time estimates, risks, and a checklist to turn this into a full SOP package."

This elevates your SOP into a polished operations asset.

Common Mistakes to Avoid

- Writing steps that are too broad ("format book")
- Leaving ownership ambiguous
- Forgetting to include quality checks
- Not updating SOPs as workflows evolve
- Overcomplicating the language
- Writing SOPs you never actually use

A great SOP is simple enough to follow and strong enough to ensure consistency.

Template You Can Reuse

"Create an SOP with:

- Purpose
- Scope
- Responsibilities
- Steps
- Quality checks

Workflow: [paste]."

Speed Tip
Add: "Then convert this into a clean, copy/paste checklist format."

This gives you both the SOP and a fast-use version.

29. Workflow Simplification

Prompt
"Simplify this workflow by removing unnecessary steps, reducing complexity, and identifying the fastest path to the same outcome. Provide: (1) the streamlined version, (2) what to remove, (3) risks, and (4) speed boosters. Workflow: [paste workflow]."

Why It Works
Most workflows become cluttered over time. New steps are added "just in case." Old steps remain even when they are no longer needed. People patch problems instead of redesigning the process. Eventually, the process becomes slow, frustrating, and overly complicated.

This prompt cuts through all of that.

It forces the model to:

- Identify the minimum viable steps needed to achieve the same outcome
- Remove redundancies, bottlenecks, and friction points
- Highlight risks of over-removal so you stay safe
- Provide speed boosters (automation, shortcuts, sequencing changes)

This is exactly how operational efficiency consultants think—streamline first, optimize second. The result is a workflow that's faster, cleaner, easier to teach, and easier to follow.

When to Use It

Use this prompt when:

- A process feels too slow or frustrating
- You want to reduce workload without sacrificing quality
- You're overwhelmed by complexity
- You're preparing for growth or scaling
- You're auditing workflows for automation
- You want to shorten turnaround time
- You're simplifying home or work routines
- You're mapping processes for outsourcing

Especially powerful for:

- Content creation
- Email and admin routines

- Book production
- Hiring and onboarding
- Client delivery
- Marketing
- Household systems
- Event planning

Anything repeated should be simplified.

Examples

Example 1 — Social Media Workflow

Input
Workflow: brainstorm → script → design → edit → schedule → post → track analytics

Output
Streamlined Version:

- Brainstorm 10 ideas
- Turn top 3 into posts (skip scripting unless long form)
- Use templates for design
- Schedule all at once
- Review analytics weekly
- Remove:
    - Scripting every post
    - Daily posting
    - Editing multiple rounds
- Risks:
    - Losing depth on long form content

- Reduced experimentation

Speed Boosters:

- Use AI for idea → caption
- Batch tasks
- Auto-publish tools

Example 2 — Household Management

Input
Workflow: plan meals → make list → shop at two stores → prep produce → cook daily → weekly cleanup

Output
Streamlined Version:

- Choose 3 repeating meals per week
- Auto-generate grocery list
- Shop once
- Prep produce on Sunday
- Cook in batches
- Quick nightly clean

Remove:

- Two-store shopping
- Daily extensive cooking

Risks:

- Less variety
- Need good storage

Speed Boosters:

- Pre-chopped produce
- Meal rotation system

Example 3 — Book Publishing

Input
Workflow: outline → draft → edit → revise → edit again → format → upload → proof → revise → publish

Output
Streamlined Version:

- Outline
- Write clean first draft
- One full developmental edit
- One line edit
- Format
- Proof + publish

Remove:

- Multiple unnecessary editing rounds
- Redundant revisions

Risks:

- Rushing structural issues
- Missing a professional edit

Speed Boosters:

- AI-supported developmental pass
- Template-based formatting

- Set strict editing boundaries

Variations

- Ultra-simple version: "Reduce to the absolute minimum 3–5 steps."
- Delegation version: "Simplify for handing off to a VA or contractor."
- Automation-first: "Rewrite workflow to maximize automation."
- Low-energy version: "Simplify steps for someone with limited bandwidth."
- High-accuracy version: "Simplify without risking quality."

Pro Difficulty Upgrade

Ask the model to include:

- a before-and-after comparison table
- estimated time saved
- unnecessary decision points
- a minimal version, standard version, and upgraded version
- automation tools or AI prompts
- bottlenecks + fixes
- dependencies you can eliminate
- the 20% of steps that produce 80% of results

Example enhancement:

"Add a before/after table and list the highest-ROI improvements."

This transforms streamlining into strategic optimization.

Common Mistakes to Avoid

- Keeping steps that exist only out of habit
- Overcomplicating simple tasks
- Writing workflows that only you can follow
- Adding safety steps that don't actually improve quality
- Confusing thoroughness with effectiveness
- Assuming old processes still make sense

Simplification is not cutting corners—it's removing friction.

Template You Can Reuse
"Simplify this workflow. Provide: Streamlined version, what to remove, risks, speed boosters, workflow: [paste]."

Speed Tip
Add: "Now turn the simplified version into a one-page SOP."

This gives you both a new process and documentation in minutes.

30. Meeting Agenda Builder

Prompt
"Create a clear, time-bound meeting agenda with: (1) purpose, (2) topics in logical order, (3) owner for each item, and (4) time limits. Make it realistic and focused. Meeting details: [paste context or goals]."

Why It Works
Bad meetings happen for one reason:
unclear structure.

People show up not knowing:

- the goal
- what will be decided
- what needs to be discussed
- how long each topic should take

- who leads each part

As a result, meetings tend to drift, digress, and balloon into unproductive conversations that waste time and cause confusion. A strong agenda changes everything. It defines boundaries, clarifies purpose, and provides each attendee with a clear mental map of what to expect.

This prompt quickly produces a professional-grade agenda that:

- Defines the meeting's purpose
- Orders the discussion in a logical flow
- Assigns owners so responsibility is clear
- Includes time limits to prevent drift
- Builds in decision points

The result is a meeting that runs smoothly, ends on time, and produces actual outcomes—not vague chatter.

When to Use It

Use this prompt when:

- You're planning a meeting
- You want to avoid wasted time
- You need clarity on what's being decided
- You're leading a team or project discussion
- You're facilitating a client or stakeholder meeting
- You're preparing for a weekly check-in

- You need structure for a difficult conversation
- You want attendees to come prepared
- You need a repeatable template

Especially helpful for:

- Project kickoffs
- Strategy meetings
- Editorial or content planning
- Book development meetings
- One-on-ones
- Team check-ins
- Leadership updates
- Family planning or logistics talks

A meeting with a clear agenda is 5x more productive.

<u>Examples</u>

Example 1 — Project Check-In

Input
Meeting details: weekly project sync

Output
Purpose: Align on progress and unblock issues.
Agenda:

- Quick wins + updates (Owner: team, 5 min)
- Blockers to resolve (Owner: PM, 10 min)

- Decisions needed this week (Owner: Lead, 10 min)
- Next steps + owners (Owner: PM, 5 min)

Total Time: 30 minutes

Example 2 — Client Meeting

Input
Meeting details: presenting a draft proposal

Output
Purpose: Review proposal and align on revisions.

Agenda:

- Overview of proposal (You, 5 min)
- Walkthrough of key sections (You, 10 min)
- Client questions (Client, 10 min)
- Revision decisions (Joint, 10 min)
- Next steps + timeline (You, 5 min)

Total Time: 40 minutes

Example 3 — Book Development Meeting

Input
Meeting details: planning next chapters

Output
Purpose: Align on chapter direction and assign writing tasks.

Agenda:

- Review progress on previous chapters (Author, 5 min)
- Discuss goals for next section (Author, 10 min)
- Brainstorm chapter themes (Team, 10 min)
- Assign writing tasks (Author, 5 min)
- Timeline + check-in schedule (Author, 5 min)

Total Time: 35 minutes

Variations

- Minimalist: "Create a 10-minute agenda with only 2 topics."
- Deep-dive: "Create a 90-minute agenda with breaks."
- Decision-heavy: "Highlight decisions to be made in bold."
- Conflict-sensitive: "Add guardrails to prevent derailment."
- Workshop: "Include activities and time for breakout discussions."
- One-on-one: "Add check-in, goals, feedback, support, and action items."

Pro Difficulty Upgrade

Ask the model to include:

- materials attendees should review beforehand
- questions to think about prior to the meeting
- risks of not covering certain topics

- discussion prompts
- a follow-up email template
- a summary script for the meeting facilitator
- a version optimized for hybrid or remote meetings

Example enhancement:

"Add pre-read materials, discussion prompts, and a follow-up email."

This turns your agenda into a complete meeting workflow.

Common Mistakes to Avoid

- Cramming too many items into one meeting
- Leaving time allocations vague
- Not specifying who leads each section
- Mixing decisions, updates, and brainstorming in one block
- Not preparing pre-read materials
- Letting minor topics take over
- Ending without next steps and owners

A meeting without structure is a conversation with no destination.

Template You Can Reuse

"Create a time-bound agenda with:

- Purpose

- Topics in order
- Owner per item
- Time limits

Meeting details: [paste]."

Speed Tip

If you want to automate your meetings, add:

"Now produce the follow-up summary I can send after the meeting."

Chapter 5 — Personal Life (10 Prompts)

Personal life workflows—meals, shopping, health routines, travel, finances, family communication—quietly consume hours every week. This section removes that friction.

Each prompt turns everyday tasks into streamlined systems so you gain back time, mental bandwidth, and emotional energy. The goal: reduce cognitive load, eliminate decision fatigue, and build simple, repeatable routines for a smoother life.

31. Meal Planning

Prompt
"Create a simple weekly meal plan with: (1) 5–7 meals, (2) variety but low effort, (3) a balanced mix of protein/veg, and (4) ingredients that overlap to reduce shopping time. Dietary notes: [paste preferences/restrictions]."

Why It Works
Meal planning is one of the most time-consuming mental tasks in daily life. You're not just deciding what to eat—you're juggling:

- preferences
- dietary needs
- what's in the pantry

- time constraints
- energy levels
- overlapping ingredients
- waste reduction

This prompt removes that mental juggling. It creates a seamless plan that combines variety with efficiency. Instead of starting from scratch every week, you receive a curated selection of meals, designed to:

- minimize prep
- reduce decision fatigue
- use overlapping ingredients
- keep nutrition steady
- reduce shopping trips
- avoid food waste

This is the same approach used by nutrition coaches and time-management experts: choose a few simple, rotating meals instead of reinventing everything every day.

When to Use It

Use this prompt when:

- You want a fast, automatic meal plan
- You're overwhelmed by daily decision-making
- You want healthier meals without complexity
- You're on a budget or don't want waste

- You need meals that fit your schedule and energy levels
- You want to streamline grocery shopping
- You're planning meals for a partner or family
- You're doing meal prep or batch cooking

It is especially helpful if you're managing:

- Chronic illness or low-energy days
- ADHD or executive function challenges
- Caregiving
- Busy work schedules
- Rotating work weeks
- Kids or family meals

This prompt helps you feed yourself well with minimal mental effort.

Examples

Example 1 — Low-Effort Balanced Meals

Input
Dietary notes: no restrictions, low-effort dinners

Output
Weekly Meal Plan:

- Rotisserie chicken + bagged salad
- Sheet-pan chicken + broccoli
- Turkey tacos
- Pasta with jarred sauce + spinach

- Stir fry (frozen veg + chicken strips)
- Breakfast-for-dinner (eggs + toast + fruit)
- Leftovers night

Overlapping Ingredients:

- chicken (rotisserie + sheet-pan + stir fry)
- spinach/bagged greens for multiple meals
- tortillas used in tacos + breakfast wraps

Example 2 — Vegetarian

Input
Dietary notes: vegetarian, simple prep

Output
Weekly Meal Plan:

- Lentil soup
- Veggie stir fry with tofu
- Pasta primavera
- Veggie-loaded omelet
- Black bean quesadillas
- Roasted vegetable bowls
- Avocado toast + fruit

Overlapping Ingredients:

- spinach
- bell peppers
- onions
- beans
- tortillas

Example 3 — Family-Friendly

Input
Dietary notes: picky kids, 30-minute meals

Output
Weekly Meal Plan:

- Chicken quesadillas
- Baked spaghetti
- Sliders + sweet potato fries
- Breakfast-for-dinner
- BBQ pulled chicken sandwiches
- DIY pizza night
- Leftovers

Overlapping Ingredients:

- tortillas
- shredded cheese
- ground beef/turkey
- marinara

Variations

- Budget version: "Focus on low-cost staples under $2/serving."
- Anti-decision fatigue: "Make 3 rotating meals for the whole week."
- High-protein: "Prioritize lean protein and quick prep."
- Batch-cook: "Choose meals that reheat well."

- Low-energy days: "Plan meals that require <10 minutes of effort."
- Healthy snacks: "Add 5 simple snacks that fit the plan."
- Family edition: "Include kid-friendly sides."

Pro Difficulty Upgrade

Ask the model to add:

- a complete grocery list
- prep instructions for Sunday
- storage instructions
- substitutions for allergies
- macro breakdown
- one "no-cook" emergency meal
- one "freezer-friendly" meal
- time estimates
- steps to reduce cleanup

Example enhancement:

"Add grocery list, prep guide, and 2 no-energy backup meals."

This turns meal planning into a fully automated routine.

Common Mistakes to Avoid

- Picking meals that require too many unique ingredients

- Overplanning (you don't need 7 new meals every week)
- Ignoring low-energy days
- Forgetting leftovers
- Planning meals no one actually likes
- Trying to cook like a chef on weeknights
- Making shopping lists after planning (instead of integrated)

Simplicity is the key to long-term consistency.

Template You Can Reuse
"Create a weekly meal plan with:
• 5–7 meals
• Low effort
• Overlapping ingredients
• Balanced nutrition
Dietary notes: [paste]."

Speed Tip
Add: "And convert this into a grocery list by store section."

This eliminates wandering through the aisles.

32. Grocery Automation

Prompt
"Create an automated grocery system based on this weekly meal plan. Include: (1) a categorized shopping list, (2) recurring staples, (3) optional

add-ons, and (4) time-saving substitutions. Meal plan: [paste or describe].”

Why It Works

Grocery shopping isn’t just the trip to the store—it’s the constant cycle of:

- remembering what you need
- checking what you have
- comparing meal ingredients
- deciding what’s worth buying
- managing fridge space
- making sure nothing goes to waste

This is why meal planning often falls apart: the grocery list becomes the bottleneck.

This prompt turns your meal plan into a repeatable grocery system—not just a list. The model organizes ingredients into simple store categories, adds your recurring staples automatically, and includes substitutions to save time, money, or energy.

You move from thinking about groceries to simply executing a clear, reusable plan.

When to Use It

Use this prompt when:

- You want frictionless grocery shopping

- You want to reduce time spent wandering aisles
- You want to avoid forgotten items
- You want a consistent weekly or biweekly routine
- You're planning meals for a partner or family
- You have limited energy for decision-making
- You're setting up a recurring grocery delivery order
- You want a "set-and-forget" household system

Especially helpful if:

- You have executive function challenges
- You're managing a chronic illness or low energy days
- You're managing for groceries as a caregiver
- You rely on grocery pickup or delivery
- You want to automate regular purchases

This prompt creates a household workflow that practically runs itself.

<u>Examples</u>

Example 1 — Based on a Simple Meal Plan

Input

Meal plan: rotisserie chicken, pasta night, turkey tacos, stir fry, breakfast-for-dinner

Output
Categorized Shopping List
Produce:

- Broccoli
- Spinach
- Bell peppers
- Onions

Protein:

- Rotisserie chicken
- Ground turkey
- Eggs

Pantry:

- Pasta
- Jarred sauce
- Tortillas
- Rice
- Stir fry sauce

Dairy:

- Shredded cheese
- Milk

Recurring Staples

- Olive oil
- Salt/pepper
- Coffee/tea

- Snacks

Optional Add-Ons

- Frozen fruit
- Salad kits
- Pre-chopped veg

Time-Saving Substitutions

- Pre-cooked chicken strips instead of raw chicken
- Heat-and-eat rice instead of traditional rice
- Bagged greens instead of whole heads of lettuce

Example 2 — Vegetarian Version

Input
Meal plan: lentil soup, veggie stir fry, pasta primavera, black bean quesadillas, roasted veg bowls

Output
Categorized Shopping List
Produce:

- Carrots
- Spinach
- Bell peppers
- Zucchini
- Sweet potatoes

Protein:

- Lentils
- Black beans
- Tofu

Pantry:
- Pasta
- Tortillas
- Vegetable broth
- Olive oil

Dairy (optional):
- Cheese for quesadillas

Recurring Staples
- Spices
- Onions
- Garlic

Substitutions
- Frozen veg mix for stir fry
- Canned lentils for faster soup
- Pre-cubed sweet potatoes

Example 3 — Family Version

Input
Meal plan: sliders, spaghetti, quesadillas, pizza night, BBQ chicken sandwiches

Output
Categorized Shopping List:

- Produce: onions, bagged salad, fruit
- Meat: ground beef, chicken breasts
- Pantry: marinara, buns, tortillas, BBQ sauce
- Dairy: shredded cheese, mozzarella
- Frozen: fries, pizza dough (optional)

Recurring Staples:

- Yogurt
- Cereal
- Snacks

Substitutions:

- Frozen chicken strips for faster sandwiches
- Pre-made pizza crusts

Variations

- Budget version: "Optimize for cost—use store brands."
- Healthy version: "Make swaps that increase nutrition."
- Low-energy: "Prefer no-chop, no-cook ingredients."
- Delivery-ready: "Format list for Instacart/Amazon Fresh."
- Bulk prep: "Add bulk ingredients for batch cooking."
- Two-person household: "Shrink portions and reduce waste."

Pro Difficulty Upgrade

Ask the model to include:

- a "default weekly list" you can reuse
- biweekly staples vs. weekly perishables
- a pantry inventory template
- recommended storage methods
- a "use-this-up" list to reduce food waste
- reminders for rotating stock
- estimated cost per category

Example enhancement:

"Add a recurring default list + storage tips + a use-this-up plan."

This turns grocery shopping into a fully automated system.

Common Mistakes to Avoid

- Creating a new list from scratch every week
- Forgetting staples (coffee, oil, spices, snacks)
- Overbuying produce that spoils quickly
- Ignoring what's already in the pantry
- Buying ingredients that don't overlap
- Planning meals with completely different ingredient sets
- Not building in substitutions or backups

Automation only works if the system is repeatable.

Template You Can Reuse

"Create an automated grocery system with:

- Categorized shopping list
- Recurring staples
- Optional add-ons
- Time-saving substitutions

Based on this meal plan: [paste]."

Speed Tip

Add: "Now format this as a digital checklist I can reuse weekly."

The model will give you a simple list you can check off on your phone.

33.Health Habit Tracking

Prompt

"Create a simple health habit tracker based on my goals. Include: (1) 3–5 habits, (2) daily checkboxes, (3) weekly summary questions, and (4) low-energy modifications. Goals: [paste your health goals]."

Why It Works

Health habits often fail not because people don't care, but because the system demands too much thinking. Most tracking apps overwhelm you with metrics, charts, reminders, badges, and friction. The brain disengages when a habit needs too much setup or mental effort.

This prompt creates a minimalist, low-friction habit system that:

- tracks only what matters
- removes overwhelm
- adapts to low-energy days
- keeps habits visible and actionable
- builds momentum without pressure
- rewards consistency, not perfection

By narrowing the focus to 3–5 habits, you avoid habit fatigue. Adding low-energy alternatives ensures you can stay consistent even if you're tired, sick, or overloaded.

The weekly reflection questions help you adjust the system in real time. You get clarity, momentum, and accountability with zero complexity.

When to Use It

Use this prompt when:

- You want to build or rebuild healthy routines
- You want tracking that doesn't feel exhausting
- You're managing chronic illness or fluctuating energy
- You want a lightweight system, not an app
- You're structuring habits around work and life demands

- You want to stay consistent without pressure
- You're tracking progress over time

Especially powerful for:

- Sleep
- Hydration
- Stretching
- Gentle movement
- Meditation
- Medication routines
- Mental health habits
- Nutrition
- Rest and recovery

This is a system designed for real-life consistency, not unrealistic discipline.

<u>Examples</u>

Example 1 — General Health Goals

Input
Goals: drink more water, move daily, improve sleep

Output
Daily Habits:
☐ Drink 64 oz water
☐ 10-minute walk or stretch
☐ No screens 30 min before bed

Low-Energy Versions:

- 5 sips of water every hour
- 3-minute stretch
- Swap "no screens" for "dim screens" on tough days

Weekly Summary:

- What helped me feel best this week?
- What drained me?
- One adjustment for next week?

Example 2 — Managing Chronic Illness

Input
Goals: gentle activity, hydration, pacing

Output
Daily Habits:

☐ Salt/electrolytes

☐ Gentle movement (5–10 min)

☐ Pacing breaks (3x/day)

☐ Consistent wake time

Low-Energy Versions:

- Electrolytes only (skip full water intake)
- Seated stretching
- 2-minute recline instead of full pacing break
- Wake within 1-hour window

Weekly Summary:

- How was my energy?
- Did pacing prevent crashes?
- What signals did I notice?

Example 3 — Weight-Loss or Strength Goal

Input
Goals: portion control, strength 3x/week, steps 6k/day

Output
Daily Habits:
☐ High-protein breakfast
☐ Hit 6,000 steps
☐ Track one meal (not all)

Low-Energy Versions

- Protein shake instead of meal
- 3,000 steps or paced indoor laps
- Track only protein intake

Weekly Summary

- What was easiest?
- What was hardest?
- One improvement?

Variations

- Habit stacking: "Group habits into morning, afternoon, evening."

- Mood tracking: “Add a 1–5 mood check line.”
- Sleep-focused: “Prioritize sleep routine + wind-down habits.”
- Fitness: “Add sets, reps, or movement minutes.”
- Nutrition: “Add simple nutrition markers.”
- Mental wellness: “Add gratitude or stress checks.”

Pro Difficulty Upgrade

Ask the model to include:

- progress milestones
- triggers and reminders
- habit resets for bad weeks
- a monthly review template
- color-coded categories (sleep, movement, mood, nutrition)
- a “non-negotiable one thing” for every day
- weekly habit difficulty adjustment

Example enhancement:

“Add triggers, a monthly check-in, and a fallback version for high-stress weeks.”

This turns the tracker into a long-term behavior system.

Common Mistakes to Avoid

- Tracking too many habits (creates burnout)
- Using an app that overwhelms you
- Tracking without adjusting based on feedback
- Choosing habits that require high energy daily
- Starting with the hardest habits first
- Skipping low-energy alternatives

Consistency is built on doing something, not everything.

Template You Can Reuse
"Build a health habit tracker with:
• 3–5 daily habits
• Low-energy versions
• Weekly reflection
Based on these goals: [paste]."

Speed Tip
Add: "Turn this into a printable 1-page tracker."

The model will format it like a clean calendar or checklist.

34. Sleep Optimization Notebook

Prompt
"Create a simple sleep optimization notebook with: (1) a nightly checklist, (2) a morning reflection, (3)

low-energy options, and (4) one weekly insight summary. Tailor this to my sleep goals: [paste your goals]."

Why It Works

Sleep issues are rarely just about sleep—they're about systems. Most people depend on willpower ("I'll go to bed earlier tonight"), but sleep only improves when tracked gently and consistently.

A sleep notebook works because it:

- surfaces patterns you don't notice
- reduces decision fatigue at night
- shortens the wind-down process
- reinforces recovery habits
- helps you understand what improves or disrupts sleep
- adapts to low-energy days
- keeps the system simple enough to stick with

Instead of overwhelming you with data or apps, this prompt creates a simple, human-focused sleep log—a structure you can keep up with even when you're tired or distracted. The system supports you without becoming another task.

When to Use It

Use this prompt when:

- You're trying to improve sleep quality or duration
- You want a simple evening routine
- You experience insomnia, disrupted sleep, or inconsistent nights
- You want to identify what helps or hurts your sleep
- You want a low-friction way to track patterns
- You want sleep routines that work regardless of energy levels

Particularly effective for:

- Early wake-ups
- Racing mind at night
- Stress or overwhelm
- No wind-down routine
- Nighttime screen use
- Inconsistent bedtimes

This notebook turns sleep into a predictable, supportive routine.

<u>Examples</u>

Example 1 — General Sleep Goals

Input
Goals: go to bed earlier, reduce screen time, sleep more consistently

Output
Nightly Checklist (10 minutes):
☐ Dim lights
☐ No screens 30 minutes before bed
☐ Light stretch or breathing
☐ Prep water + phone charger
☐ Set tomorrow's top 3 tasks

Low-Energy Versions:
- Screens → switch to warm/dim mode
- Stretch → 1-minute neck/shoulder release
- Top 3 tasks → choose just 1

Morning Reflection:
- Sleep quality (1–5)
- What helped last night?
- What disrupted sleep?
- Mood/energy upon waking

Weekly Insight: "One thing that consistently improves my sleep…"

Example 2 — Chronic Illness

Input
Goals: improve restorative sleep, reduce crashes, maintain consistent routine

Output
Nightly Checklist:

☐ Gentle wind-down (5 min)
☐ Hydration + electrolytes
☐ 2–3 paced breathing cycles
☐ Cool room + comfortable pillows
☐ Light reading or low-demand activity

Low-Energy Versions:

- Breathing → simply recline in dim light
- Hydration → small sips instead of full bottle
- Reading → audiobook or calm sound
- Morning Reflection:
- Restorative level (1–5)
- Energy baseline
- Orthostatic symptoms
- Was pacing effective yesterday?

Weekly Insight: "What consistently leads to better recovery?"

Example 3 — High-Stress Work Week

Input
Goals: reduce late-night anxiety, improve morning alertness

Output
Nightly Checklist:
☐ Write down 3 worries (close browser afterward)
☐ Set alarm + avoid scrolling
☐ 10 deep breaths

☐ Warm shower or face rinse

☐ Room temp check

Low-Energy Versions:

- 3 worries → jot down 1
- Deep breaths → 3 breaths only
- Shower → warm washcloth

Morning Reflection:

- Wake mood
- First thought of the day
- Stress level (1–5)
- Anything that helped lower anxiety?

Weekly Insight:
"What triggered stress most often, and how did I respond?"

Variations

- Productivity version: "Add morning focus prompts."
- Couples: "Include shared routines."
- Parents: "Add kid routines and flexibility."
- Shift workers: "Adapt to irregular schedules."
- Travel: "Add jet lag adjustments."
- Biohacker: "Add temperature, supplements, and light exposure tracking."

Pro Difficulty Upgrade

Ask the model to include:

- pre-bed rituals based on your chronotype
- environmental checklist (light, noise, temp)
- stress triggers and coping tools
- weekly graphs or patterns
- a "sleep-saving fallback plan" for bad nights
- gentle morning activation (light, hydration, breathing)
- rules for screens, caffeine, alcohol

Example enhancement:

"Add a fallback plan for nights when I know I won't sleep well."

This builds resilience into the system.

Common Mistakes to Avoid

- Trying 20 new habits at once
- Overtracking (apps, devices, multiple logs)
- Skipping low-energy modifications
- Getting discouraged by bad nights
- Forcing unrealistic bedtimes
- Ignoring lifestyle rhythm (light exposure, screens, caffeine)

A sleep system works only if it's simple enough to repeat nightly.

Template You Can Reuse
"Create a sleep optimization notebook with:

- Nightly checklist
- Morning reflection
- Weekly insight

Goals: [paste]."

Speed Tip
Add: "Turn this into a printable one-page sleep journal."

The model will format it as a clean grid or checklist.

35. Vacation Planning

Prompt
"Plan a simple, stress-free vacation with: (1) 2–3 destination options, (2) a 3–5 day itinerary, (3)

estimated costs, and (4) packing essentials. Preferences: [paste trip details]."

Why It Works

Planning a vacation should feel exciting—but in reality, it's often overwhelming. You have to decide:

- where to go
- how long to stay
- what to do
- where to eat
- how to budget
- what to pack
- what to book first
- how to avoid overplanning or overspending

Even a short getaway can turn into a long list of decisions that create stress instead of joy.

This prompt streamlines everything into a ready-to-use plan so you skip the cognitive load and get straight to enjoyment. It gives you:

- Destination options tailored to your preferences
- A realistic itinerary that balances activity and rest
- Cost estimates so you can budget confidently
- A packing list that prevents last-minute stress

Whether you want a relaxing retreat, a family trip, or an adventure weekend, this prompt builds a frictionless plan you can execute instantly.

When to Use It

Use this prompt when:

- You're planning a vacation or weekend getaway
- You want options before committing
- You're overwhelmed by details
- You want to avoid travel fatigue or decision overload
- You want a simple trip with minimal logistics
- You need a family-friendly or budget-friendly plan
- You're planning for low energy or physical limitations
- You want clarity on costs before booking anything

Especially helpful for:

- Couples trips
- Solo escapes
- Family vacations
- Road trips
- City weekends
- Beach retreats
- Nature trips

This makes travel planning effortless.

<u>Examples</u>

Example 1 — Relaxing 3-Day Beach Trip

Input
Preferences: relaxing, beach, low activity, warm weather, minimal planning

Output
Destination Options:

- San Diego
- Gulf Shores
- Charleston beaches

3-Day Itinerary:
Day 1:

- Arrive, check in
- Walk on the beach
- Casual dinner nearby

Day 2:

- Slow morning + coffee
- Beach time (umbrella/chair rental)
- Afternoon nap or pool
- Sunset dinner

Day 3:

- Brunch
- Short local sightseeing

- Head home

Estimated Cost:

- Hotel: $150–$250/night
- Food: $40–$70/day
- Activities: $25–$60

Packing Essentials:

- Sunscreen
- Hat + swimsuit
- Sandals
- Kindle/book
- Refillable water bottle

Example 2 — Family-Friendly Weekend Trip

Input
Preferences: two adults + two kids, budget-friendly, fun activities, short drive

Output
Destination Options:

- Local waterpark resort
- Nearby national/state park
- City with children's museum

3-Day Itinerary:
Day 1:

- Drive
- Check in
- Pool or park afternoon

Day 2:

- Kid-friendly attraction (museum, zoo, aquarium)
- Lunch
- Afternoon rest
- Evening movie or board games

Day 3:

- Breakfast
- Short activity
- Drive home

Estimated Cost:

- Hotel: $120–$180/night
- Activities: $15–$40 per person
- Food: $60–$100/day

Packing Essentials:

- Snacks
- Water bottles
- Kid outfits + backup clothes
- Chargers
- Entertainment for car

Example 3 — Adventure Weekend

Input
Preferences: hiking, outdoors, moderate challenge, minimal gear

Output
Destination Options:

- Sedona
- Lake Tahoe
- Boulder

Itinerary:
Day 1: travel + easy hike
Day 2: main hike (4–6 hours)
Day 3: brunch + scenic drive

Packing Essentials:

- Hiking shoes
- Light layers
- Hydration pack
- Snacks
- Sunglasses

Variations

- Luxury version: "Include upgraded hotels, spas, and fine dining."
- Budget-conscious: "Keep the trip under $500 total."
- Low-energy/medical: "Minimize walking + include rest breaks."
- Solo traveler: "Focus on easy navigation and safety."
- International: "Add passport reminders and key phrases."
- Road trip: "Add mileage, rest stops, and roadside attractions."

- Outdoor: “Include gear list + weather checks.”

Pro Difficulty Upgrade

Ask the model to include:

- hotel options with pros/cons
- restaurant suggestions
- reservation timelines
- accessibility notes
- weather considerations
- a “prep checklist” for the week before
- an emergency plan
- one splurge option and one budget option

Example enhancement:

“Add hotel suggestions, a prep list, and three restaurant options per day.”

This builds a fully ready-to-book travel guide.

Common Mistakes to Avoid

- Overplanning (leads to burnout)
- Underplanning (leads to stress)
- Forgetting transportation timing
- Packing too much
- Choosing a destination misaligned with energy level
- Not budgeting properly

- Trying to do too many activities

A good vacation is simple, calm, and intentional.

Template You Can Reuse
"Plan a vacation with:

- 2–3 destination options
- 3–5 day itinerary
- Cost estimates
- Packing essentials

Preferences: [paste]."

Speed Tip
Add: "Now turn this into a bookable checklist with the 5 things I need to reserve first."

This prevents planning bottlenecks.

36. Contractor Comparison

Prompt
"Compare contractors for this project. Provide: (1) a simple comparison table, (2) pros/cons for each contractor, (3) red flags, and (4) a recommendation with explanation. Project: [paste details]. Options: [paste contractor names or descriptions]."

Why It Works
Hiring a contractor is stressful because it's a mix of:

- money

- trust
- risk
- quality control
- timelines
- communication style

And most people don't have a framework for evaluating contractors beyond "who seems nicest" or "who gave the lowest bid."

This prompt produces a structured, decision-ready comparison that highlights:

- Key differences
- Quality indicators
- Pricing transparency
- Red flags
- The contractor most aligned with your goals

It removes emotional guesswork and brings clarity to a decision that could otherwise cost thousands of dollars and months of frustration.

When to Use It

Use this prompt when:

- You're comparing estimates or bids
- You want clarity before hiring
- You're choosing between contractors with different specialties
- You're evaluating home repairs, remodeling, or improvement projects

- You’re choosing a service provider (plumber, electrician, landscaper, etc.)
- You feel unsure how to weigh cost vs. quality
- You need a clean summary to discuss with a partner
- You're trying to avoid scams or low-quality work

Especially helpful for:

- Roofers
- Painters
- Electricians
- Plumbers
- General contractors
- Landscapers
- HVAC techs
- Flooring installers
- Solar companies
- Pool contractors

This prompt turns a stressful decision into a grounded one.

<u>Examples</u>

Example 1 — Two Contractors for Bathroom Remodel

Input
Project: small bathroom remodel

Options: A (mid-range), B (low-cost)

Output

Comparison Table

Comparison Table

Factor	Contractor A	Contractor B
Price	$$	$
Timeline	3 weeks	5+ weeks
Quality	High	Mixed
Warranty	1 year	None
Reviews	Excellent	Few reviews
Communication	Strong	Inconsistent

Pros/Cons

A – Pros: reliable, quality work, clear timeline
A – Cons: higher price

B – Pros: low cost
B – Cons: unclear timeline, no warranty, limited references

Red Flags

- B: No written warranty
- B: Inconsistent communication
- B: Low estimate without detail

Recommendation: Choose Contractor A for long-term reliability and fewer risks.

Example 2 — Landscaping Quotes

Input
Project: backyard clean-up and new sod
Options: Contractor GreenLeaf, Contractor SunRise

Output

Comparison Table

Factor	GreenLeaf	SunRise
Price	Mid	High
Timeline	2 days	1 day
Add-ons	Irrigation check included	Irrigation extra
Reviews	Good	Excellent

Pros/Cons

- GreenLeaf: Good price, slower timeline
- SunRise: Fast, very high quality but more expensive

Recommendation: Choose SunRise if speed and precision matter; choose GreenLeaf if budget matters more.

Example 3 — Painter Quotes

Input
Project: interior painting

Options: ProColor vs. BudgetBrush

Output
Red Flags

- BudgetBrush uses sub-contractors with unclear oversight
- ProColor: none

Recommendation: ProColor offers better oversight, quality assurance, and warranty.

Variations

- Three+ contractors: "Add all options to the comparison table."
- Budget-focused: "Highlight total cost + hidden fees."
- Quality-focused: "Weight quality and experience most heavily."
- Timeline-focused: "Prioritize who can finish fastest with least disruption."
- Risk-first: "List biggest risks for each contractor."
- Decision matrix: "Add scoring 1–5 for each criterion."
- Partner communication: "Rewrite as a simple 1-page summary for my spouse."

Pro Difficulty Upgrade

Ask the model to include:

- weighted scoring matrix (importance by category)
- cost breakdown (materials vs. labor)
- negotiation tips
- questions to ask during the next call
- a "scam check" list
- what should be included in the contract
- photo checklist for documenting work
- timeline expectations + milestone payments

Example enhancement:

"Add negotiation tips, red flags, and questions to ask before signing."

This turns the comparison into a full contractor hiring playbook.

Common Mistakes to Avoid

- Choosing based solely on lowest bid
- Not verifying licenses or insurance
- Not asking for references
- Ignoring communication problems
- Forgetting to check warranty details
- Not getting a detailed written estimate
- Paying too much upfront
- Not setting clear expectations on cleanup and final walk-through

Contract decisions should be based on clarity, not charisma.

Template You Can Reuse
"Compare these contractors and provide:

- Comparison table
- Pros/cons
- Red flags
- Recommendation

Project: [paste]
Options: [paste]."

Speed Tip
Add: "Turn this into a side-by-side graphic summary I can screenshot."

The model will format it into a clean, visual layout.

37. Budget Snapshot

Prompt
"Create a simple budget snapshot with: (1) income summary, (2) fixed expenses, (3) variable expenses, (4) monthly surplus/deficit, and (5) 2–3 improvement recommendations. My details: [paste your numbers]."

Why It Works
Most budgeting tools fail because they're too complex. They require categories, subcategories,

percentage rules, tracking every purchase, syncing accounts, and constant maintenance. That level of granularity overwhelms people—not because they don't want to budget, but because the tools create friction.

This prompt gives you a clean, one-page snapshot that answers the only questions that matter:

- What's coming in?
- What's going out (fixed vs. variable)?
- What's left?
- Where can improvements be made fast?

It avoids guilt, math, and endless spreadsheets—while still providing clarity. It also distinguishes fixed from variable, which is essential for understanding where change is possible. This prompt is simple on purpose. Simplicity = consistency.

When to Use It

Use this prompt when:

- You want a fast overview of your financial situation
- You're deciding whether you can afford something
- You want to cut spending without tracking every penny
- You're aligning finances with a partner

- You're trying to prioritize savings or debt repayment
- You're overwhelmed by budgeting apps
- You want a monthly check-in system that's quick

Especially helpful for:

- Tight budgets
- Busy schedules
- Executive function challenges
- Shared household finances
- Unexpected expenses
- Lifestyle adjustments
- Annual planning

This is budgeting for real life—not for perfect discipline.

<u>Examples</u>

Example 1 — Single Adult

Input
Income: $4,500/month
Fixed: rent $1,600, insurance $200, phone $70, car $350
Variable: groceries $400, dining $250, gas $150, fun $200, misc $150

Output
Income: $4,500

Fixed Expenses: $2,220
Variable Expenses: $1,150
Total Monthly Expenses: $3,370
Surplus: $1,130

Recommendations:

- Redirect $300–$500/month into savings or debt.
- Cap dining at $150 to boost surplus.

Example 2 — Couple With Kids

Input
Income: $7,200
Fixed: mortgage $2,400, utilities $300, insurance $350, childcare $1,200
Variable: groceries $700, kid activities $200, gas $250, dining $300, misc $300

Output
Income: $7,200
Total Expenses: $6,000
Surplus: $1,200

Recommendations:

- Automate $500 savings.
- Reduce dining by $100 to build a buffer for kids' activities.

Example 3 — Tight Budget

Input
Income: $3,000
Fixed: $1,900
Variable: $800

Output
Surplus: $300

Recommendations:

- Lower variable spending to $600.
- Re-shop insurance and phone plans.

Variations

- Debt-focused: "Add minimum payments and fastest payoff path."
- Savings-focused: "Add emergency fund recommendations."
- Household: "Create separate snapshots for each partner + combined."
- Business owner: "Separate personal vs. business expenses."
- Simplicity-first: "Reduce categories to 5 total."
- Planning version: "Create a 6-month projection."

Pro Difficulty Upgrade

Ask the model to include:

- a 50/30/20 breakdown

- high/medium/low priority spending categories
- a "no-guilt" discretionary allowance
- 3 easy savings wins
- subscription audit
- upcoming annual expenses
- stress-test scenarios ("What if income drops 10%?")
- a quick plan to increase surplus

Example enhancement:

"Add a priority ranking and three ways to reduce expenses without changing lifestyle."

This transforms your snapshot into a strategic plan.

Common Mistakes to Avoid

- Tracking too many categories
- Forgetting irregular or annual expenses
- Focusing on tiny expenses instead of big ones
- Ignoring fixed vs. variable differences
- Trying to overhaul everything at once
- Treating budgets as punishment instead of clarity
- Not reviewing once a month

A budget snapshot is about awareness, not control.

Template You Can Reuse
"Create a budget snapshot with:

- Income
- Fixed expenses
- Variable expenses
- Surplus/deficit
- Recommendations

My details: [paste]."

Speed Tip
Add: "Now turn this into a printable one-page monthly budget sheet."

It creates a reusable personal finance dashboard.

38. Gift Ideas

Prompt
"Give me personalized gift ideas for this person. Include: (1) 5–7 options at different price points, (2) why each gift fits their personality, (3) one sentimental option, (4) one practical option. Person details: [paste description]."

Why It Works
Gift-giving is a mental load problem disguised as generosity. You're juggling:

- personality
- interests
- budget
- age

- lifestyle
- what they already own
- what feels meaningful
- what feels appropriate

That's why people procrastinate or default to generic options (gift cards, candles, random objects). This prompt gives you tailored, thoughtful ideas in minutes by analyzing the person's traits the way a professional gift curator would.

The structure matters:

- 5–7 ideas → enough variety without overwhelm
- Different price points → flexibility for your budget
- Why it fits → confidence that the gift will land
- Sentimental + practical options → two categories people value most

This eliminates decision fatigue and delivers gifts that feel personal instead of obligatory.

When to Use It

Use this prompt when:

- A birthday, holiday, or anniversary is approaching
- You're stuck and can't think of anything

- You want the gift to feel meaningful
- The person “already has everything”
- You’re shopping for someone hard to please
- You want something non-generic
- You need fast inspiration before a deadline
- You’re organizing a gift for a group

Especially helpful for:

- Partners
- Parents
- In-laws
- Kids and teens
- Bosses or colleagues
- Friends
- Teachers
- Clients
- Neighbors

This turns a stressful decision into a thoughtful plan.

<u>Examples</u>

Example 1 — For a Book-Loving Friend

Input
Person: loves reading, minimalistic, enjoys quiet nights, introverted, mid-30s

Output
Gift Ideas

- Personalized bookmark engraved with initials
  Why it fits: Minimalistic but meaningful.

- Subscription to a curated book box
  Why: Gives them new authors without decision fatigue.

- High-quality reading lamp
  Why: Improves nighttime reading.

- A book annotated by you
  Sentimental: Adds personal meaning.

- Digital library card + audiobook credits
  Why: Perfect for exploring new authors and multitasking

Example 2 — For a Teenager

Input
Person: 15-year-old, into music, TikTok, hoodies, tech gadgets

Output

- Portable mini Bluetooth speaker
- Trending oversized hoodie
- LED room strip lights
- Gift card to a sneaker or streetwear shop

- Custom playlist you make (sentimental)
- Phone lens kit for video content (practical)

Example 3 — For a Grandparent

Input
Person: 70s, sentimental, loves family stories, enjoys gardening

Output
- Photo book of family memories (sentimental)
- Personalized garden tools
- Monthly seed subscription
- Digital photo frame preloaded with pictures
- Garden kneeler + seat combo (practical)
- Handwritten letter with a favorite shared memory

Variations
- Budget version: "Keep all options under $25."
- Luxury version: "Include premium splurge items."
- Experience-focused: "Focus on shared or local experiences."
- Last-minute: "Ideas available same-day or digital."
- Minimalist: "Choose clutter-free gifts."

- Kids: “Include developmental or creativity-based options.”
- Coworker: “Neutral gifts that work professionally.”
- Pets: “Gift ideas for pet lovers.”

Pro Difficulty Upgrade

Ask the model to include:

- a ranking from best → least strong
- a “safe” option if you’re unsure
- a wow-factor option
- sentimental message ideas
- a custom card note
- linked themes (book lover, traveler, foodie, etc.)
- matching add-ons (e.g., candle + bath salts)

Example enhancement:

“Rank the ideas and add a card message for the top pick.”

This makes the gift ready to give—emotionally and practically.

Common Mistakes to Avoid

- Buying something generic
- Choosing based on your preferences, not theirs

- Getting things that add clutter
- Overthinking it
- Giving items with complicated setup or maintenance
- Ignoring sentimental potential
- Giving items that feel impersonal
- The best gifts are thoughtful, not extravagant.

Template You Can Reuse
"Give gift ideas for: [paste person]. Include:

- 5–7 options
- Why each fits
- Sentimental option
- Practical option."

Speed Tip
Add: "Now create one top pick and the exact message to write in the card."

It removes the final barrier to giving the gift.

39. Family Communication Helper

Prompt
"Help me communicate this message clearly and kindly to my family. Provide: (1) a short script, (2) a gentle but firm version, (3) a boundary-setting version, and (4) one follow-up message if needed. Context: [paste situation]."

Why It Works

Family communication is one of the hardest communication categories because it's layered with:

- history
- emotion
- habits
- assumptions
- old patterns
- unspoken expectations

When you're emotionally invested, it becomes extremely difficult to write a message that is:

- clear
- calm
- respectful
- boundaries-based
- free of guilt, blame, or escalation

This prompt gives you emotionally intelligent communication with multiple tone options, so you can choose what fits the moment. It also prepares a follow-up message—critical when someone doesn't respond the way you hope.

By separating "short," "gentle," and "boundary-setting," you get emotional distance and clarity that's almost impossible to produce on your own when you're in the middle of family dynamics.

When to Use It

Use this prompt when:

- you need to communicate difficult news
- you're setting a boundary
- you're clarifying expectations
- you want to avoid conflict
- you want to soften a message without losing clarity
- you need to respond to someone who is upset
- you're preparing for a family gathering
- you're dealing with miscommunication or tension
- you want to reduce emotional labor
- you want to break old communication patterns

Especially helpful for:

- parents
- siblings
- adult children
- in-laws
- blended families
- co-parenting
- extended family group chats

Family communication often needs clarity plus kindness—this prompt provides both.

Examples

Example 1 — Declining an Invitation

Input
Context: declining a family gathering without hurting feelings

Output
Short Version:

> "Thank you for the invite. I won't be able to make it this time, but I hope everyone has a great day."

Gentle Version:

> "I really appreciate you inviting me. I'm keeping things quieter right now and won't make it, but I'm thinking of you and hope it's a wonderful gathering."

Boundary-Setting Version:

> "I'm limiting commitments right now for my own wellbeing. I won't be able to attend, but thank you for understanding."
>
> Follow-Up (if pressured):
> "I know it may be disappointing, but my decision is firm. I care about you, and this is what I need right now."

Example 2 — Asking for More Help

Input
Context: needing siblings to contribute more to parent care

Output
Short Version:

> "We need to rebalance responsibilities. Can we divide tasks more evenly?"

Gentle Version:

> "I appreciate everything you do. Things have become overwhelming on my end, and I need us to share the responsibilities more evenly. Could we review the weekly tasks together?"

Boundary Version:

> "I can no longer sustain the current load. Starting next week, I need each of us to take on defined tasks so care is not falling on one person."
>
> Follow-Up:
> "I'm not asking out of frustration—I'm asking because this isn't sustainable. We're all in this together."

Example 3 — Addressing Hurt Feelings

Input
Context: a relative said something hurtful

Output

Short Version:

"I wanted to share that the comment yesterday hurt my feelings."

Gentle Version:

"I know it wasn't intentional, but the comment yesterday really affected me. I care about our relationship and wanted to share that honestly."

Boundary Version:

"Comments like that are hurtful and I need them to stop. I want to continue our relationship respectfully."

Follow-Up:

"I'm glad we talked. I'm moving forward, and I appreciate your willingness to understand."

Variations

- Co-parenting: "Add a neutral tone to avoid escalation."
- In-law dynamics: "Add extra diplomacy."
- Adult children: "Keep it supportive but firm."
- Holiday planning: "Create a group message + expectations."
- Family crisis: "Add clarity and reassurance."

- Apologies: "Add versions that take responsibility without over-owning."
- Direct confrontation: "Add a stronger boundary section."

Pro Difficulty Upgrade

Ask the model to include:

- an "if they react badly…" response
- a version that reduces guilt
- tone options (warm, neutral, concise, humorous)
- phrases to avoid
- phrases that calm conflict
- a 30-second phone-call script
- a summary sentence to stay grounded
- an escalation plan if disrespect continues

Example enhancement:

"Give me scripts, phrases to avoid, and a follow-up message if they push back."

This turns the prompt into a communication toolkit.

Common Mistakes to Avoid

- over-explaining
- apologizing for setting boundaries

- responding emotionally instead of intentionally
- assuming the person will react badly
- trying to fix their feelings
- using vague language
- mixing multiple messages in one text
- delaying the conversation out of anxiety

Clear, kind, concise messages reduce 80% of family conflict.

Template You Can Reuse
"Help me communicate this message to my family. Provide:

- short script
- gentle script
- boundary-setting script
- follow-up message

Context: [paste]."

Speed Tip
Add: "Now rewrite the best version so it sounds exactly like me."

This makes the message authentic and natural.

40. Memory Capture Journaling

Prompt
"Help me capture this memory in a way that's vivid, simple, and emotionally true. Provide: (1) a

short version, (2) an expanded narrative, (3) a future-me reflection, and (4) 3 prompts to deepen the memory. Memory: [paste details]."

Why It Works

Most people lose 90% of their meaningful memories because they don't have a system to capture them. Journaling often feels intimidating:

- too long
- too emotional
- too much pressure
- too many blank pages
- don't know what to say
- don't know what matters

This prompt bypasses all of that by giving you a guided, effortless structure that turns any moment—small or big—into a vivid, preserved memory.

It works because it:

- Captures the facts (what happened)
- Captures the feeling (why it mattered)
- Captures the insight (how it shaped you)
- Creates future perspective (what future-you will want to remember)

It transforms vague moments into meaningful record. It also reduces the emotional barrier: you don't have to "journal," you just respond.

This is memory-keeping for busy, overwhelmed, or low-energy lives.

When to Use It

Use this prompt when:

- Something meaningful happened and you don't want to forget
- You want to capture moments with kids, partners, friends, or paren
- You're trying to track emotional patterns
- You want to remember wins or milestones
- You're journaling for self-growth
- You're processing grief, change, or transition
- You want material for a memoir or future writing
- You want to build gratitude without forced positivity

Especially helpful for:

- Daily life moments
- Memories of loved ones
- Travel
- Holidays
- Career milestones
- Personal breakthroughs
- Childhood or family history

This creates a record your future self (and possibly your family) will cherish.

Examples

Example 1 — Small Joy

Input
Memory: my morning coffee on the porch today felt unusually peaceful

Output
Short Version:

> "Quiet morning, warm mug, cool air. Nothing urgent. Just peace."

Expanded Narrative:

> "This morning I sat on the porch with my coffee and noticed how calm everything felt. The light was soft, the air was cool, and for once my brain wasn't racing. It felt like a small reset—one of those rare moments where time slows down."

Future-Me Reflection:

> "Remember: peace often comes in ordinary moments, not dramatic changes."

Deepening Prompts:

- What detail do you want to remember forever?
- What made this moment feel different?
- What did your body feel like?

Example 2 — Important Conversation

Input
Memory: my daughter told me she was proud of me

Output
Short Version:

> "She said she was proud of me—and it landed deeper than I expected."

Expanded Narrative:

> "When my daughter told me she was proud of me, I felt something shift. It wasn't dramatic, but it was grounding. I realized she sees me trying, even when I feel like I'm barely holding things together. Her words felt like permission to keep going."

Future-Me Reflection:

> "When doubt shows up again, remember this moment: you are seen."

Deepening Prompts:

- What tone of voice did she use?
- What did you feel in your chest or stomach?
- How did this change the rest of your day?

Example 3 — Travel Memory

Input
Memory: walking through Florence at sunset

Output
Short Version:

> "Florence glowed gold. I felt incredibly alive."

Expanded Narrative:

> "The Florence sunset felt unreal—warm light spilling over the river, the sounds of footsteps on stone, the faint smell of bread and wine drifting through the streets. It felt like stepping into a painting. For a moment, everything felt aligned."

Future-Me Reflection:

> "You are someone who comes alive in beauty and movement—don't forget that."

Deepening Prompts:

- What did you hear, smell, taste?
- Who were you with and how did you feel together?
- What does this place represent in your life?

Variations

- Grief journaling: "Add gentle guidance and grounding."

- Parenthood journaling: “Add prompts that capture growth over time.”
- Relationship journaling: “Add emotional nuance and appreciation.”
- Creative journaling: “Add sensory detail prompts.”
- Trauma-aware: “Emotionally safe version—no assumptions.”
- Memoir-prep: “Ask deeper questions about context and change.”
- Tiny moments: “Capture micro-memories in under 3 sentences.”

Pro Difficulty Upgrade

Ask the model to include:

- sensory details (5-sense recall)
- emotional anchors
- a one-sentence theme
- metaphor or imagery
- what this memory teaches you
- how it might shape future decisions
- a photo caption (if you want to pair the memory with images)
- a gratitude line that’s not forced

Example enhancement:

“Add sensory details and give me three possible themes for the memory.”

This deepens meaning without making it heavy.

Common Mistakes to Avoid

- Trying to write "perfectly"
- Overexplaining instead of feeling
- Avoiding emotional truth
- Writing too abstractly ("it was nice")
- Forgetting why the moment mattered
- Thinking small memories aren't important
- Waiting until you have time (you won't)

Your real life is made of tiny, powerful moments. Capture them before they fade.

Template You Can Reuse
"Help me capture this memory. Include:

- short version
- expanded narrative
- future reflection
- 3 prompts
- Memory: [paste]."

Speed Tip
Add: "Now create a yearly memory log format using this structure."

The model will turn your journaling into a long-term keepsake system.

Chapter 6 —Learning & Growth (10 Prompts)

The fastest way to improve your work, habits, and thinking is through continuous learning. However, most people learn reactively and inefficiently.

They chase tutorials, skim articles they forget, highlight books they don't reread, and believe that more information leads to better understanding. It doesn't.

This section reframes learning as a system. The aim is to leverage AI to speed up understanding, eliminate confusion, and turn knowledge into actionable skills. These prompts focus not on studying harder but on extracting meaning more quickly, organizing information neatly, and developing skills gradually.

You'll see prompts that simplify complex ideas, convert raw data into usable insight, build micro-courses, break down mistakes, check your thinking for bias, and create growth plans you can sustain. The consistent purpose across all of them is leverage: less time consumed, more learning retained, and clearer thinking with less effort.

The tools here support long-term development. They help you think more critically, learn new skills with intention, and operate with a clearer understanding of what matters and why. The effect compounds: better insights drive better decisions, which drive better outcomes.

41. Book Summary

Prompt
"Give me a clear, accurate book summary with: (1) main argument, (2) 5 key insights, (3) notable quotes or ideas, and (4) how to apply the lessons. Book: [paste title and author]."

Why It Works
Most people want to read more but don't. The issue isn't time; it's retention. After finishing a book, especially nonfiction, many readers:

- forget the core argument
- lose track of key ideas
- never apply any of it
- struggle to articulate what they learned
- mix it up with other books

This prompt solves all of that by creating a structured, high-retention summary that distills the book into its most valuable components.

The structure ensures you retain:

- The main argument — what the book is really about
- Key insights — what matters, not the filler
- Notable ideas/quotes — memorable anchors
- Applications — how to actually use the knowledge

This converts a passive reading experience into active, useful learning.

It's also invaluable when you:
- want to preview a book before reading
- want to remember a book you read years ago
- want to share the ideas with someone
- want to decide whether a book is worth buying
- want a quick refresher for writing or research

This prompt turns books into actionable knowledge.

When to Use It

Use this prompt when:
- Starting a new book and want a preview
- Finishing a book and want retention
- Deciding whether to buy/read a book
- Researching for writing or speaking
- Summarizing books for newsletters or reports

- Comparing several books in a niche
- Creating your personal knowledge library
- Recalling key ideas from old favorites

It's especially powerful for:

- Nonfiction
- Self-help
- Business
- Psychology
- Leadership
- History
- Productivity
- Personal development
- Spirituality
- Creativity

This prompt elevates your reading from information intake to transformation.

Examples

Example 1 — "Atomic Habits" byJames Clear

Input
Book: Atomic Habits by James Clear

Output
Main Argument: Small, consistent habits compound into remarkable long-term change.

5 Key Insights:

- Systems > Goals
- Identity-based habits are the strongest
- Make habits obvious, attractive, easy, satisfying
- Environment shapes behavior more than motivation
- Continuous improvement beats intensity

Notable Ideas:

- "You do not rise to the level of your goals. You fall to the level of your systems."
- Habit stacking for momentum

Applications:

- Choose one identity-based habit to build
- Remove friction from good habits
- Add friction to bad habits

Example 2 — "The Body Keeps the Score" by Bessel van der Kolk

Input
Book: The Body Keeps the Score

Output
Main Argument: Trauma reshapes the brain and body; healing requires mind-body integration.

5 Key Insights:

- Trauma affects physiology, not just memory
- Talk therapy alone isn't enough

- Somatic practices relieve stored stress
- Safety is the foundation of healing
- Community accelerates recovery

Notable Ideas:
- Neuroplasticity enables healing
- Yoga and movement support trauma recovery

Applications:
- Explore grounding techniques
- Build supportive relationships
- Incorporate body-based practices

Example 3 — "Daring Greatly" by Brené Brown

Input
Book: Daring Greatly

Output
Main Argument: Vulnerability is the path to courage, connection, and meaningful living.

5 Key Insights:
- Shame thrives in secrecy
- Vulnerability requires boundaries
- Courage is a practice, not a trait
- Perfectionism blocks authenticity
- Connection is built through openness

Applications:

- Practice small acts of vulnerability
- Name shame triggers
- Replace perfection with "good enough"

Variations

- Short version: "Keep it under 150 words."
- Ultra-short: "Summarize in 5 bullet points total."
- Academic: "Add theoretical frameworks."
- Business: "Add leadership and workplace applications."
- Spiritual: "Add reflective questions."
- Compare: "Compare this book to [another title]."
- Contrarian: "What does the author miss?"
- Relevance: "Explain why this book matters today."

Pro Difficulty Upgrade

Ask the model to include:

- a 30-second elevator summary
- the book's target audience
- blind spots or criticisms
- how the ideas evolved over time
- one metaphor that captures the book
- a "memory hook" sentence
- how to apply the ideas this week
- a 3-layer summary (10-word, 50-word, 250-word versions)

Example enhancement:

"Give me 10-word, 50-word, and 250-word summaries for retention."

This creates multi-level mastery and deeper understanding.

Common Mistakes to Avoid

- Treating summaries like book replacements (they aren't)
- Focusing on plot over theme (for nonfiction)
- Forgetting application
- Overloading with details
- Mixing your interpretation with the book's argument
- Losing the author's intent
- Summarizing ideas without organizing them

A great summary clarifies—not complicates.

Template You Can Reuse
"Summarize this book with:

- Main argument
- 5 key insights
- Notable ideas/quotes
- Applications

Book: [paste title]."

Speed Tip

If you want fast recall after reading, add: "Now give me the 10 most memorable lines or lessons."

42. Article Synthesis

Prompt
"Synthesize these articles into one clear, coherent summary with: (1) the shared argument, (2) 5–7 combined insights, (3) points of disagreement, and (4) what the reader should take away. Articles: [paste links or text]."

Why It Works
Information overload is now the default. You're constantly absorbing:

- news
- commentary
- expert essays
- research papers
- think pieces

- blog posts
- newsletters
- policy reports

But the human brain isn't built to naturally merge multiple sources into a unified understanding. Instead, you get:

- fragmented takeaways
- competing ideas
- "I read something but forgot what"
- too much noise, not enough signal

This prompt converts multiple sources into ONE cohesive mental model, the way an analyst or researcher would.

It helps you see:

- Core themes across sources
- What matters most
- Where authors agree
- Where they disagree
- What the big-picture insight actually is

This dramatically increases retention and gives you a clear perspective in a world drowning in content.

When to Use It

Use this prompt when:

- Researching a topic
- Preparing to write or speak on an issue

- Comparing viewpoints
- Reading several articles on the same subject
- Trying to understand a complex topic
- Studying for school or work
- Sorting out contradictory information
- Building background knowledge
- Summarizing curated newsletters
- Processing multiple think-tank reports

Especially helpful for:

- Politics
- Technology
- AI
- Public policy
- Economics
- History
- Health
- Social issues
- Science and research

This prompt turns scattered information into clarity.

Examples

Example 1 — AI Regulation Articles

Input
Articles: The Atlantic, MIT Technology Review, NYT (AI ethics/regulation pieces)

Output

Shared Argument: AI is advancing faster than existing regulation, creating gaps in safety, accountability, and democratic oversight.

Combined Insights:

- Governments lack the technical talent to regulate effectively.
- Companies self-regulate unevenly, prioritizing speed over safety.
- Transparency standards vary widely.
- Ethical frameworks exist, but enforcement is inconsistent.
- Public trust depends on clear guardrails.
- International cooperation is necessary.

Points of Disagreement:

- How urgent the risks are
- Whether regulation should be industry-led or government-led
- How much innovation regulation might stifle

Takeaway: Regulation must catch up, but it must be done intelligently—with technical expertise and global coordination.

Example 2 — Economic Outlook Articles

Input

Articles: WSJ, Vox, Bloomberg on inflation decline

Output
Shared Argument: Inflation is easing but underlying economic tensions remain.

Combined Insights:

- Labor markets are still tight.
- Consumer demand remains strong.
- Supply chains have mostly normalized.
- Core inflation is slower to fall.
- Housing costs distort the headline numbers.

Points of Disagreement:

- Timing of rate cuts
- Whether the soft landing is secure
- Long-term risk assessment

Takeaway: The economy is improving, but the recovery is uneven and fragile.

Example 3 — Parenting Articles

Input
Articles: 3 blog posts about screen time for kids

Output
Shared Argument: Screens aren't inherently harmful, but intentional boundaries matter.

Combined Insights:

- Models of behavior matter
- Quality content beats quantity
- Co-viewing improves outcomes
- Predictable routines reduce conflict
- Parents' stress level is a bigger factor than screen time itself

Disagreement: Some experts push strict limits; others emphasize flexibility.

Takeaway: Balance and consistency work better than rigid rules.

Variations

- Deep research: "Add citations + differences in methodology."
- Compare more sources: "Synthesize 5–10 articles."
- Critical lens: "Add what's missing from these arguments."
- Action-based: "Add what I should do with this information."
- Opposing viewpoints: "Highlight ideological differences."
- Timeline version: "Show how the narrative changed over time."

Pro Difficulty Upgrade

Ask the model to include:

- a comparative matrix
- contradictions between authors
- where evidence is strong vs. weak
- what's speculation vs. fact
- implications for the future
- questions the topic raises
- risks and opportunities
- a 1-paragraph "executive interpretation" written in your voice

Example enhancement:

"Add contradictions, future implications, and a one-paragraph final interpretation."

This builds a high-level analytical synthesis—ideal for authors and researchers.

Common Mistakes to Avoid

- Treating multiple articles as equal (they aren't)
- Confusing opinions with data
- Losing the big picture
- Letting one source dominate unfairly
- Focusing too much on details
- Ignoring bias or assumptions
- Mixing unrelated content

Good synthesis clarifies the whole, not the parts.

Template You Can Reuse
"Synthesize these articles with:

- shared argument
- 5–7 combined insights
- disagreements
- takeaway

Articles: [paste]."

Speed Tip
If you want to process a large reading list fast, add: "Now create a one-page research brief in bullet form."

43. Teach Me in My Learning Style

Prompt
Teach me this concept in my learning style. Give: (1) a simple explanation, (2) an analogy tailored to my style, (3) a visual or step-by-step breakdown, (4) an example, and (5) a quick quiz. Learning style: [paste your style]. Concept: [paste concept]."

Why It Works
Learning isn't just about absorbing information—it's about receiving it in the format your brain prefers.

Everyone learns differently, but most explanations assume:

- high energy
- strong attention spans

- perfect comprehension
- a love of dense text

That's unrealistic. This prompt acts as a translator, adapting information into the specific form that fits your brain, not a generic one.

It works because it:

- Simplifies the idea into a single clear explanation
- Maps it to your learning style (visual, auditory, kinesthetic, narrative, logical, low-energy, high-speed, etc.)
- Uses analogy, the fastest way humans understand abstract ideas
- Gives examples, which anchor meaning
- Adds a quick quiz, which boosts retention by 30–70%

This turns confusing or abstract ideas into clean, accessible learning moments.

When to Use It

Use this prompt when:

- you're learning something new
- you're overwhelmed by a topic
- the explanation you read didn't stick
- you want mastery, not memorization
- you have low energy and need simplicity

- you're preparing for a test, meeting, or project
- you need to teach someone else
- you want to understand fast without losing depth

Especially powerful for:

- technology
- AI and machine learning
- finance
- biology
- politics
- history
- psychology
- productivity concepts
- math and data
- new work skills

This prompt uses your learning strengths instead of fighting your weaknesses.

<u>Examples</u>

Example 1 — For a Visual Learner

Input
Learning style: visual
Concept: inflation

Output

Simple Explanation: Inflation is when the price of things goes up over time, reducing how much your money can buy.

Analogy: Think of your money as a balloon. Over time, the balloon slowly deflates while prices inflate around it.

Visual Breakdown (step-by-step):
Year 1: $10 = 10 apples
Year 3: $10 = 8 apples
Year 5: $10 = 6 apples

Example: If your rent went from $1,200 to $1,350, that's inflation.

Quick Quiz: If prices rise 10%, how much does a $100 item cost?

Example 2 — For a Narrative Learner

Input
Learning style: storytelling
Concept: compound interest

Output
Simple Explanation: Compound interest means your money grows on itself—interest on interest.

Analogy (story): Imagine planting one apple tree. The next year, that tree produces apples that become new trees. Then those trees grow more trees. Your money spreads like an orchard.

Narrative Example: Maria invests $1,000. After a year, it becomes $1,050. The next year, interest grows on $1,050—not just the original $1,000. Her orchard expands forever.

Quick Quiz:Why does waiting extra years dramatically increase growth?

Example 3 — For a Low-Energy Learner

Input
Learning style: low-energy, brain fog
Concept: photosynthesis

Output
Simple Explanation (20 words): Plants use sunlight to turn air and water into food. Sunlight = power, leaves = kitchen, sugar = food.

Analogy: A leaf is a tiny solar-powered kitchen.

Step Breakdown:

- Sunlight hits leaf
- Leaf grabs CO_2
- Roots grab water
- Leaf mixes them into sugar
- Oxygen released

Quick Quiz: What two ingredients does the plant pull in?

Variations

- Speed learning: "Explain in under 100 words."
- Deep dive: "Explain in stages: beginner → intermediate → advanced."
- Kid-friendly: "Teach like I'm 10 years old."
- Executive briefing: "Explain like I need to present this at work in 2 minutes."
- Exam-prep: "Add sample test questions."
- Creative: "Explain using a metaphor only."
- Plain language: "Avoid all jargon."
- Neurodivergent-friendly: "Use ultra-clear, step-by-step logic."

Pro Difficulty Upgrade

Ask the model to include:

- multiple analogies so you can choose the best
- a diagram (ASCII or described)
- a one-minute teaching script
- a troubleshooting guide ("what confuses most people")
- misconceptions to avoid
- 3 signals you fully understand the concept
- a "teach it back to me" final step

Example enhancement:

"Give me two analogies, a sample diagram, and one misconception to avoid."

This transforms the explanation into a full learning tool.

Common Mistakes to Avoid

- Overcomplicating the concept
- Jumping straight into jargon
- Letting the explanation be too long
- Skipping the analogy
- Giving only one example
- Confusing details with understanding
- Ignoring your actual learning style
- Trying to memorize instead of internalize

The goal isn't memorization—it's comprehension.

Template You Can Reuse

"Teach me this concept in my learning style with:

- simple explanation
- tailored analogy
- visual/step breakdown
- example
- quick quiz
- Learning style: [paste]
- Concept: [paste]."

Speed Tip

Add: "Now give me a version I can explain to someone else in 20 seconds."

This creates instant mastery.

44. Micro-Course Creation

Prompt
"Create a micro-course on this topic. Include: (1) a 5-lesson structure, (2) learning objectives for each lesson, (3) a simple exercise per lesson, (4) a final assessment, and (5) next-steps for continued learning. Topic: [paste topic]. Audience: [paste audience]."

Why It Works
People rarely need a full course: they need a compact, practical, high-retention learning path they can finish quickly. Micro-courses work because they:

- reduce overwhelm
- break learning into digestible chunks
- create a sense of completion
- provide immediate application
- adapt to any skill level
- avoid academic jargon
- turn knowledge into action fast

Most online courses over-teach. This prompt avoids that by forcing the model to prioritize:

- 5 essential lessons

- Clear outcomes
- Short, doable exercises
- A simple assessment
- Actionable next steps

You get a structured learning experience without hours of videos or pages of content. This approach turns any topic into a mini-curriculum you can complete in one sitting—or spread over a week.

When to Use It

Use this prompt when:

- You want to learn a new skill quickly
- You're researching a topic for work or writing
- You're teaching someone else (kids, team, clients)
- You want a self-paced study plan
- You need foundational understanding fast
- You want to create educational content
- You're preparing for a speech, workshop, or training
- You want to build a knowledge library

Especially helpful for:

- AI + tech skills
- Writing + communication
- Productivity methods
- Psychology and personal development
- Health and wellness topics

- History/politics backgrounders
- Research frameworks
- Creative skills

Micro-courses turn scattered knowledge into structured mastery.

Examples

Example 1 — Micro-Course on Habit Building

Input
Topic: habit building
Audience: beginners

Output
Lesson 1 — How Habits Work
Objective: understand cues, routines, rewards
Exercise: list 3 habits + their cues

Lesson 2 — Identity-Based Habits
Objective: choose the identity behind the habit
Exercise: write "I am the kind of person who…"

Lesson 3 — Make Habits Easy
Objective: reduce friction
Exercise: modify one habit so it takes < 2 minutes

Lesson 4 — Track Lightly
Objective: use simple tracking
Exercise: check off a 3-day streak

Lesson 5 — Build Momentum
Objective: pair habits and stack
Exercise: stack one habit after something you already do

Final Assessment: Explain one habit you built and why it worked.

Next Steps: Try habit stacking, environment design, or adding accountability.

Example 2 — Micro-Course on AI Basics

Input
Topic: artificial intelligence
Audience: non-technical adults

Output
Lesson 1 — What AI Is
Objective: understand basic definitions
Exercise: rewrite the definition in your own words

Lesson 2 — How AI Learns
Objective: understand datasets + training
Exercise: identify 3 everyday examples

Lesson 3 — What AI Can Do
Objective: see real-life applications
Exercise: list 5 tasks AI could do for you

Lesson 4 — Limits of AI
Objective: understand accuracy and bias
Exercise: find one example of AI making an error
Lesson 5 — Using AI Safely
Objective: know when to trust vs. verify
Exercise: create a personal AI safety rule

Final Assessment: Explain AI to a 10-year-old in 3 sentences.

Next Steps: Explore prompt engineering or automation.

Example 3 — Micro-Course on Writing a Memoir

Input
Topic: memoir writing
Audience: first-time writers

Output
Lesson 1 — The Purpose of a Memoir
Exercise: write a one-sentence memoir theme

Lesson 2 — Finding Your Core Story
Exercise: list 5 pivotal life moments

Lesson 3 — Voice + Tone
Exercise: write a paragraph in your natural voice

Lesson 4 — Structure
Exercise: outline 3 possible story arcs

Lesson 5 — Begin Drafting
Exercise: draft your first page

Final Assessment: Write a 300-word scene based on a real memory.

Next Steps: Begin chapter outlines and scene logs.

Variations

- Kids version: "Make it kid-friendly + activity-based."
- Advanced: "Add deeper readings and challenges."
- Corporate: "Add workplace application + team exercises."
- Creative: "Add visual or storytelling elements."
- Speed-learning: "Create a 30-minute condensed version."
- Low-energy: "Add tiny, 1-minute exercises."
- Assessment-heavy: "Add quizzes for each lesson."
- Workshop: "Turn it into a 60-minute teachable session."

Pro Difficulty Upgrade

Ask the model to include:

- prerequisite knowledge

- misconceptions to avoid
- a capstone project
- difficulty escalations
- sample scripts for teaching
- resource recommendations
- a pacing guide (1 day, 1 week, 1 month)
- checkpoint questions

Example enhancement:

"Add a capstone project and a pacing guide."

This makes the micro-course fully ready for teaching or self-study.

Common Mistakes to Avoid

- Lessons that are too long
- Advanced concepts added too early
- Too many exercises
- Overpacking content
- Trying to master everything at once
- No practical application
- No assessment → no retention

Micro-courses work because they stay small and focused.

Template You Can Reuse

"Create a micro-course with:

- 5 lessons

- objectives
- exercise per lesson
- final assessment
- next steps

Topic: [paste]
Audience: [paste]."

Speed Tip
Add: "Now turn this into a printable one-page PDF-style outline."

The model will format a clean, structured course sheet.

45. Skill Roadmap

Prompt
"Create a skill roadmap for mastering this skill. Include: (1) beginner → intermediate → advanced stages, (2) 3–5 milestones per stage, (3) learning resources, (4) practice exercises, and (5) a 30-day starter plan. Skill: [paste]."

Why It Works
Most people fail to learn new skills because the process feels:

- overwhelming
- unstructured
- unclear where to start
- unclear what "progress" looks like
- unclear what to practice

- unclear when they've leveled up

A skill roadmap solves that by breaking the entire journey into clear, achievable stages. It mirrors how professionals and instructors teach mastery:

- Beginner — foundations
- Intermediate — competence and application
- Advanced — mastery, creativity, and problem-solving

Each stage includes milestones you can see and measure, so you never wonder whether you're improving. Practice exercises ensure you build skill, not just consume content. Resources provide guidance. A 30-day plan gives you momentum.

This is how you learn any skill efficiently—coding, writing, public speaking, design, fitness, leadership, research, AI, and more.

When to Use It

Use this prompt when:

- You want to master a new skill from scratch
- You feel stuck or plateaued
- You need clarity on what to practice
- You want a realistic timeline
- You want to stop hopping between random tutorials
- You're building career, creative, or personal skills

- You want a path you can actually finish
- You want to learn strategically, not chaotically

Especially powerful for:

- technical skills
- creative skills
- athletic/physical skills
- writing and communication
- leadership and management
- entrepreneurship
- productivity systems
- research and analysis

A roadmap turns confusion into progress.

<u>Examples</u>

Example 1 — Skill: Public Speaking

Input
Skill: public speaking

Output
Beginner Stage (Weeks 1–4)
Milestones:

- Understand speech structure
- Practice 1–2 minute talks
- Reduce filler words
- Manage nerves with breathing

Exercises:
• Record yourself speaking 60 seconds daily
• Deliver a talk to a friend

Intermediate Stage (Months 2–4)
Milestones:

- Develop storytelling techniques
- Improve pacing
- Master transitions
- Engage audience

Exercises:

- Give a 5-minute talk weekly
- Rewrite a story using tension and pacing

Advanced Stage (Months 5+)
Milestones:

- Command presence
- Deliver persuasive talks
- Adapt to Q&A
- Speak without notes

Exercises:

- Present at work or community events
- Simulate hostile or complex audiences

30-Day Plan: Daily 2-minute practice, 1 weekly talk, 1 recording review.

Example 2 — Skill: Graphic Design

Input
Skill: graphic design

Output
Beginner

- Learn color, typography, composition
- Recreate simple designs

Intermediate

- Create original layouts
- Build portfolio pieces

Advanced

- Develop brand systems
- Execute complex multi-page designs

30-Day Starter Plan:
Week 1: color + typography basics
Week 2: recreate simple posters
Week 3: design 3 original pieces
Week 4: build a mini-portfolio

Example 3 — Skill: Data Analysis

Input
Skill: data analysis

Output
Beginner

- Understand datasets, spreadsheets, basic formulas

- Learn basic charts

Intermediate
- Pivot tables, dashboards, trends

Advanced
- Statistical modeling, forecasting, storytelling

30-Day Plan: Daily practice + weekly small projects.

Variations
- Career-focused: “Add job titles and income ranges.”
- Creative: “Add inspiration sources and creative drills.”
- Academic: “Add readings and research assignments.”
- Business: “Add real-world application scenarios.”
- Low-energy: “Break milestones into tiny tasks.”
- Fast-track: “Compress roadmap into 60 intense days.”
- Long-term: “Create a 12-month mastery plan.”

Pro Difficulty Upgrade

Ask the model to include:
- red flags at each stage

- common beginner mistakes
- optional advanced master paths
- a mastery benchmark (how to know you've arrived)
- a skills checklist
- a portfolio or project pipeline
- recommended mentors, communities, or forums
- a "plateau-breaking" toolkit

Example enhancement:

"Add red flags, a skills checklist, and how I'll know I've reached mastery."

This makes the roadmap comprehensive and self-correcting.

Common Mistakes to Avoid

- jumping to advanced concepts too early
- watching tutorials without practicing
- switching resources constantly
- comparing yourself to experts
- skipping fundamentals
- not measuring progress
- failing to commit to a schedule

A skill is built through repetition, clarity, and progressive challenge—not talent.

Template You Can Reuse
"Create a skill roadmap with:

- beginner → intermediate → advanced
- milestones
- resources
- exercises
- 30-day starter plan

Skill: [paste]."

Speed Tip
Add: "Now condense the roadmap into a 1-page mastery chart."

This creates a visual tracker you can use long-term.

46. Mistake Analysis

Prompt
"Help me analyze this mistake so I learn from it. Include: (1) what actually happened, (2) the root cause, (3) what I controlled vs. didn't control, (4) 3 lessons, and (5) one behavior change for next time. Mistake: [paste details]."

Why It Works
Most people reflect on mistakes emotionally, not analytically. They get stuck in:

- self-blame
- embarrassment
- rumination

- shame
- defensiveness
- avoidance

This prevents learning.

A proper mistake analysis breaks the cycle by turning a mistake into a data point, not an identity hit. The structure matters:

- What actually happened — removes dramatization
- Root cause — identifies the true driver
- Control vs. no control — removes unnecessary guilt
- Lessons — converts experience into clarity
- Behavior change — ensures forward momentum

This creates growth without self-attack. It's the same method used by:

- elite athletes
- top executives
- surgeons
- military after-action reviews
- high-performance teams

The goal is accountability without self-punishment. Clarity without shame. Progress without perfectionism.

When to Use It

Use this prompt when:

- You made an error at work
- You miscommunicated with someone
- You reacted poorly
- You feel embarrassed
- You're trying to break a habit
- Something went wrong but you don't know why
- You want to avoid repeating a pattern
- You're processing regret
- You feel stuck in rumination

Especially powerful for:

- professional mistakes
- relationship missteps
- time-management failures
- financial mistakes
- creative or writing errors
- misjudgments
- emotional reactions
- boundary lapses
- health or habit setbacks

This converts emotional noise into useful insight.

<u>Examples</u>

Example 1 — Work Mistake

Input

Mistake: I missed an important deadline and delayed the project.

Output
What Actually Happened: The timeline slipped because I underestimated the work and didn't ask for clarification.

Root Cause: Poor scoping + no checkpoints.

Control vs. No Control:

- Controlled: my planning, communication
- Not controlled: sudden priority changes

Lessons:

- Estimate using previous projects
- Set midweek checkpoints
- Ask for clear expectations

Behavior Change:

- Use a scope checklist before accepting new tasks.

Example 2 — Communication Mistake

Input
Mistake: I snapped at my partner during a stressful moment.

Output
Root Cause: Fatigue + unexpressed stress.

Lessons:

- Communicate stress earlier
- Take 30 seconds before responding
- Ask for space when overwhelmed

Behavior Change: Use a "pause phrase" like: "I want to respond, but I need a moment."

Example 3 — Habit Slip

Input
Mistake: I broke my workout streak and feel discouraged.

Output
Root Cause: Overly intense schedule → burnout.

Lessons:

- Start smaller
- Add recovery days
- Track consistency, not perfection

Behavior Change: Shift from daily workouts to 3 structured days + 2 optional.

Variations

- Leadership: "Add team impact + how to communicate next steps."
- Conflict: "Add scripts for repair conversations."

- Career: “Add professional development implications.”
- Health: “Add tracking and low-energy alternatives.”
- Creative: “Add how this affects future drafts.”
- Academic: “Add study plan improvements.”
- Neurodivergent-friendly: “Add executive-function supports.”
- Self-compassion version: “Keep tone gentle and non-judgmental.”

Pro Difficulty Upgrade

Ask the model to include:

- a timeline reconstruction
- contributing emotional triggers
- environmental factors
- blind spots you may not see
- what you did right
- how to talk about the mistake if someone asks
- a resilience plan
- a pre-mortem to prevent it next time

Example enhancement:

“Add emotional triggers, blind spots, and a pre-mortem plan.”

This turns the mistake into a professional-grade improvement loop.

Common Mistakes to Avoid

- catastrophizing
- blaming others excessively
- ignoring your role
- refusing to analyze
- seeing the mistake as identity
- trying to be perfect
- skipping the "behavior change" step
- repeating the same error

Mistakes are raw material for growth—but only if analyzed correctly.

Template You Can Reuse

"Help me analyze this mistake with:

- what happened
- root cause
- control vs. no control
- lessons
- behavior change

Mistake: [paste]."

Speed Tip

Add: "Now turn this into a 1-minute after-action ritual I can reuse."

The model will turn the analysis into a self-coaching system.

47. Bias Checking

Prompt
"Check this thinking for bias. Provide: (1) what my conclusion is, (2) potential cognitive biases influencing it, (3) alternative interpretations, (4) missing information, and (5) one balanced conclusion. Situation: [paste situation or thought]."

Why It Works
Human thinking is fast, emotional, and often pattern-driven—not logical. Even smart, self-aware people fall into predictable cognitive traps:

- confirmation bias
- negativity bias
- projection
- mind reading
- catastrophizing
- availability bias
- fundamental attribution error
- optimism bias
- overgeneralization

Biases aren't moral failures—they're shortcuts your brain takes to conserve energy.
This prompt slows your thinking down and puts it under a neutral, analytical lens.

The structure works because it:

- Clarifies your actual conclusion (most people don't articulate it)
- Identifies the relevant cognitive biases
- Presents alternative interpretations
- Highlights missing data
- Creates a balanced, grounded conclusion
- Gives you a 360° view of your own mind—without harsh judgment.
- Over time, it rewires your thinking toward accuracy, clarity, and emotional regulation.

When to Use It

Use this prompt when:

- You're spiraling about a situation
- You're interpreting someone's behavior
- You're worried you're overreacting
- You think you're underreacting
- You want a level-headed perspective
- You're making a big decision
- Something is triggering you
- You're trying to understand your emotional patterns
- You want to avoid jumping to conclusions
- You're unsure what the data actually supports

It's especially powerful for:

- relationship dynamics

- family situations
- workplace conflict
- health-related worries
- politics and news
- self-judgment
- fear, frustration, or anxiety-driven thoughts

This prompt serves as emotional fact-checking.

Examples

Example 1 — Work Scenario

Input
Situation: My boss responded curtly on Slack. I think she's angry at me.

Output
Your Conclusion: "She's upset with me."

Possible Biases:

- Mind reading
- Personalization
- Emotional reasoning
- Alternative Interpretations:
- She was multitasking
- She was in a meeting
- She was stressed about something unrelated
- That's just her communication style

Missing Information:

- Her tone with others today
- Her workload
- Any recent performance issues

Balanced Conclusion: "You might be projecting stress onto her message. Her tone may not reflect anything about you."

Example 2 — Relationship Scenario

Input
Situation: My sister didn't call me back. I think she's mad at me.

Output
Biases:

- Catastrophizing
- Personalization
- Negativity bias

Alternative Interpretations:

- She's busy
- She forgot
- She's dealing with her own stress

Balanced Conclusion: "Silence doesn't equal anger. Reach out once more and assume goodwill."

Example 3 — Self-Judgment

Input

Situation: I made a mistake at work; I think I'm terrible at my job.

Output
Biases:

- Overgeneralization
- All-or-nothing thinking
- Global labeling

Balanced Conclusion: "A mistake reflects one moment, not your overall abilities."

Variations

- Emotional version: "Add a grounding sentence to help regulate emotions."
- Analytical version: "Add probability estimates for each interpretation."
- Relationship-focused: "Add scripts for clarifying conversations."
- Decision-focused: "Add how this bias could affect my choice."
- Neurodivergent-friendly: "Use concrete, literal explanations with no assumptions."
- Workplace: "Add potential reputational or political considerations."
- Health anxiety: "Emphasize data vs. fear differences."

Pro Difficulty Upgrade

Ask the model to include:

- a ranking of the most likely interpretations
- what your emotional trigger might be
- similar past patterns that may be influencing your thinking
- a reframe that maintains truth without dismissing feelings
- one question to ask someone else to verify the situation
- the "if this were someone else" reversal
- the 10% rule ("What part is true? What part is story?")

Example enhancement:

"Add probability percentages and identify my emotional trigger."

This moves the analysis from emotional to statistically grounded.

Common Mistakes to Avoid

- assuming your first thought is the true one
- confusing feelings with facts
- skipping the "missing information" step
- interpreting silence as negativity
- projecting your internal state onto others
- mistaking patterns for evidence
- ignoring alternative explanations

Bias checking isn't about being positive—it's about being accurate.

Template You Can Reuse
"Check this thinking for bias:

- conclusion
- biases
- alternative interpretations
- missing info
- balanced conclusion

Situation: [paste]."

Speed Tip
Add: "Now rewrite the balanced conclusion into a calming, one-sentence affirmation."

This helps stabilize your emotional state quickly.

48. Data Interpretation

Prompt
"Interpret this data for me. Provide: (1) what the data actually shows, (2) trends or patterns, (3) what might be causing them, (4) what the data doesn't say, and (5) an actionable takeaway. Data: [paste table, numbers, chart, or description]."

Why It Works
Most people look at data and instantly jump to conclusions—sometimes right, often wrong.

The brain is wired to:

- see patterns (even when they aren't there)
- assume correlation = causation
- overweight dramatic data points
- ignore missing context
- read data emotionally ("this looks bad")
- misinterpret variance as trend

This prompt slows you down and forces a structured interpretation, mirroring how analysts, researchers, and decision-makers think.

It works because it:

- States only what the data truly shows
- Identifies patterns or trends
- Provides plausible causes
- Highlights what the data does not tell you (crucial)
- Gives actionable insights you can use

This prevents bad assumptions, avoids misreadings, and helps you make smart, grounded decisions. It turns raw numbers into real understanding.

When to Use It

Use this prompt when:

- reviewing business metrics
- analyzing survey responses
- looking at sales numbers

- interpreting health data
- reviewing website analytics
- analyzing polling or political data
- reviewing performance metrics
- comparing year-over-year numbers
- processing charts you don't fully understand
- trying to avoid wrong conclusions
- presenting data to others

Especially powerful for:

- entrepreneurs
- writers and researchers
- analysts
- marketers
- students
- managers
- decision-makers
- anyone processing large amounts of information

This prompt upgrades your analytical thinking instantly.

Examples

Example 1 — Marketing Data

Input
Data: website traffic down 15%, email open rate up 12%, sales steady

Output
What the Data Shows:

- Traffic declined
- Engagement with email improved
- Sales remained stable

Patterns:

- Visitors decreased, but buyers didn't
- Email list retains strong interest

Possible Causes:

- Reduced ad spend
- Seasonal dip
- Higher-quality email audience

What the Data Does Not Say:

- Whether the traffic dip is harmful
- Why people aren't visiting
- Whether sales will remain stable

Takeaway: Shift focus to email-based conversions; investigate traffic sources.

Example 2 — Personal Health Data

Input
Data: resting heart rate up 6 points this week, sleep down 45 minutes/night, steps down 20%

Output
Trends:

- Higher stress or overexertion
- Lower movement
- Reduced sleep quality

Possible Causes:
- Illness
- Busy week
- Poor sleep environment

What's Missing:
- Nutrition
- Stress level
- Hydration
- Recovery habits

Takeaway: Focus on sleep recovery first; heart rate likely normalizes afterward.

Example 3 — Sales Data

Input
Data: Q1 → \$10k, Q2 → \$12k, Q3 → \$8k, Q4 → projected \$9k

Output
Pattern: moderate volatility with no clear upward trend.

Possible Causes: seasonal demand.
Not Shown: customer acquisition cost, profit margin.

Takeaway: focus Q4 on retention and upsells.

Variations

- Advanced analysis: “Add statistical interpretations.”
- Business: “Add revenue implications + risk areas.”
- Health: “Add wellness recommendations based on trends.”
- Historical: “Explain what this means in a larger timeline.”
- Predictive: “Add a prediction for the next period.”
- Executive: “Rewrite as a board-ready insight brief.”
- Beginner-friendly: “Explain in plain language.”
- Charts: “Extract insights from the chart description.”

Pro Difficulty Upgrade

Ask the model to include:

- confidence levels (how certain each interpretation is)
- correlation vs. causation warnings
- external factors that may influence the data
- assumptions required for each conclusion
- key unknowns
- potential next tests or experiments
- a one-paragraph executive memo

- scenario planning (best case, worst case, expected case)

Example enhancement:

"Add confidence levels, assumptions, and a scenario forecast."

This turns the interpretation into a professional-grade analytical report.

Common Mistakes to Avoid

- assuming causation
- ignoring missing context
- reacting emotionally
- focusing on outliers instead of trends
- comparing mismatched timeframes
- assuming upward = good, downward = bad
- treating fluctuation as failure
- ignoring sample size
- forgetting external factors

Data only becomes dangerous when misinterpreted.

Template You Can Reuse

"Interpret this data:

- what it shows
- trends
- causes

- what's missing
- takeaway

Data: [paste]."

Speed Tip
Add: "Now turn this into a 3-bullet executive summary."

The model will compress insights into quick decision-ready clarity

49. Insight Extraction

Prompt
"Extract the key insight from this material. Provide: (1) the core idea, (2) why it matters, (3) what most people miss, (4) the simplest way to remember it, and (5) one practical application. Material: [paste text, link, notes, or idea]."

Why It Works
Reading something is easy. Understanding something is harder. But distilling something into a meaningful, usable insight is a different skill entirely.

Most people struggle because:

- They focus on details instead of meaning
- They copy quotes instead of understanding concepts

- They don’t know what the “point” actually is
- They consume content passively
- They forget the insight 2 days later
- They don’t connect new ideas to real life

This prompt sharpens your thinking by forcing the model to extract the one thing that matters: the insight that ties everything together.

It works because it:

- Identifies the core idea
- Explains why it matters (context and stakes)
- Surfaces the hidden layer—what most people miss
- Provides a memory hook
- Gives a real-world application

This turns vague content into sharp clarity, creating new neural connections and deeper understanding.

When to Use It

Use this prompt when:

- You’re reading a book or article
- You’re studying a research topic
- You’re brainstorming or problem-solving
- You’re distilling complex information
- You’re preparing notes for writing
- You’re building expertise in a field
- You’re collecting ideas for a project

- You’re overwhelmed by too much information
- You want to convert noise into signal

Especially useful for:

- nonfiction
- history
- science
- theology
- psychology
- politics
- AI + technology
- productivity and writing
- research materials
- lengthy essays

This prompt is one of the fastest ways to turn knowledge into understanding.

<u>Examples</u>

Example 1 — From a Long Article

Input
Material: a 2,000-word essay on burnout

Output
Core Idea: Burnout is not about working too much—it’s about working without meaning, rest, or agency.

Why It Matters: Fixing burnout requires structural change, not just self-care.

What Most People Miss: Burnout often comes from losing control, not from effort alone.

Memory Hook: “Exhaustion isn’t the disease—disconnection is.”

Application: Identify one task this week you can delegate, simplify, or stop altogether.

Example 2 — From Bible Verse

Input
Material: “Love your enemies…”

Output
Core Idea: Jesus reframes love as an active choice toward those who oppose us.

What Most People Miss: It’s not about passivity—it’s about breaking cycles of retaliation.

Application: Respond to one small offense with kindness instead of escalation

Example 3 — From Research Notes

Input

Material: notes about how children learn language quickly

Output
Core Idea: Kids learn languages fast because they imitate patterns, not rules.

What Most People Miss: Adults overthink grammar instead of mimicking usage.

Application: Practice by copying native phrases instead of studying grammar tables.

Variations

- Creative version: "Turn the insight into a metaphor."
- Executive version: "Make the insight actionable for leadership."
- Academic version: "Add citations and theoretical framing."
- Writer version: "Add how to use this insight in my book."
- Spiritual version: "Add a reflection question."
- Self-growth: "Add a behavior change."
- Presentation: "Turn the insight into a slide headline."
- Comparison: "Extract insights from two ideas and contrast them."

Pro Difficulty Upgrade

Ask the model to include:

- second-order insights ("What does this imply?")
- risks of misinterpreting the idea
- historical or practical context
- how the insight fits into a bigger body of knowledge
- what this insight contradicts
- a 1-sentence takeaway for teaching others
- multiple applications (work, life, relationships)

Example enhancement:

"Add second-order insights and risks of misinterpretation."

This makes the insight richer and more nuanced.

Common Mistakes to Avoid

- copying the surface-level idea
- taking quotes at face value
- missing the author's underlying argument
- collecting insights without applying them
- looking for complexity instead of clarity
- assuming the insight is obvious
- forgetting to connect it to real life

A true insight changes how you see something.

Template You Can Reuse
"Extract the insight:

- core idea
- why it matters
- what most miss
- memory hook
- application

Material: [paste]."

Speed Tip
Add: "Now give me a 10-word version I'll remember."
This creates instant retention.

50. Thirty-Day Growth Plan

Prompt
"Create a 30-day personal growth plan with: (1) one theme, (2) weekly focus areas, (3) daily micro-actions, (4) weekly reflection questions, and (5) how to measure progress. Theme: [paste your theme or goal]."

Why It Works
A 30-day window is the sweet spot for growth:

- long enough to create real behavioral change
- short enough to avoid overwhelm
- structured enough to build habit
- flexible enough to adapt

The problem: most people set goals, not systems, and goals without systems fail. This prompt creates a system-driven growth plan, not a motivational wishlist.

It works because it breaks growth into four levels:

- A single theme — keeps focus tight
- Weekly focus — creates structure without rigidity
- Daily micro-actions — frictionless steps that build momentum
- Reflection questions — consolidate learning
- Progress metrics — keep you accountable

It mirrors how top performers, athletes, and behavioral psychologists design growth cycles: small, repeatable actions with built-in feedback loops. The result: consistency instead of burnout.

When to Use It

Use this prompt when:

- You want meaningful progress fast
- You feel stuck or scattered
- You're overwhelmed and need structure
- You want to try a new habit with guardrails
- You're building a skill
- You're reshaping a mindset
- You're recovering from setbacks
- You're starting a new chapter in life

- You want a system you can repeat each month

Especially powerful for:

- Health and fitness
- Writing
- Productivity
- Emotional resilience
- Spiritual growth
- Career development
- Learning or studying
- Relationship habits
- Financial habits

This is growth in its most sustainable form.

Examples

Example 1 — Theme: "Improve My Focus"

Output
Theme: Deep focus with less distraction

Week 1 — Awareness
Daily: track distractions for 24 hours
Reflect: "When and why do I lose focus?"

Week 2 — Environment
Daily: remove one friction point
Reflect: "What small change improved focus the most?"

Week 3 — Systems
Daily: use a 25-minute focus block
Reflect: "What made focus easier today?"

Week 4 — Mastery
Daily: choose ONE task that matters most
Reflect: "Did I work on what mattered?"

Measure Progress:

- number of deep work blocks
- reduced distraction count
- subjective focus rating (1–5)

Example 2 — Theme: "Health Reset"

Output
Week 1 — Sleep
Daily: 10-minute wind-down
Reflection: "What helped me fall asleep faster?"

Week 2 — Nutrition
Daily: one high-protein meal
Reflection: "How did energy change?"

Week 3 — Movement
Daily: 10-minute walk or stretch
Reflection: "What felt easy today?"

Week 4 — Stress
Daily: 2 minutes of breathing

Reflection: “What lowered my stress?”

Progress Metrics:

- energy score
- steps or movement minutes
- sleep consistency

Example 3 — Theme: “Creative Momentum”

Output
Week 1 — Idea Capture
Daily: write 3 ideas
Reflection: “What surprised me?”

Week 2 — Drafting
Daily: write 5–10 minutes
Reflection: “What felt effortless?”

Week 3 — Editing
Daily: revise 1 small piece
Reflection: “What improved the most?”

Week 4 — Sharing
Daily: share 1 idea (post, friend, draft)
Reflection: “What was the reaction?”

Metrics:

- total drafts
- ideas generated
- consistency streak

Variations

- Business version: “Add KPIs and owner responsibilities.”
- Relationship version: “Add communication habits.”
- Healing version: “Add low-energy modifications.”
- Career version: “Add skill milestones + portfolio tasks.”
- Spiritual version: “Add reflection questions + daily presence.”
- Productivity version: “Add morning + evening resets.”
- Writer version: “Add word counts + draft progression.”

Pro Difficulty Upgrade

Ask the model to include:

- a “non-negotiable one thing” each day
- a weekly micro-challenge
- an “if I run out of energy” fallback plan
- accountability mechanisms
- a reward or milestone celebration
- a long-term continuation plan
- risk factors and how to mitigate them
- a “before/after” self-rating

Example enhancement:

"Add a fallback version and accountability system."

This makes the plan resilient and executable even during bad weeks.

Common Mistakes to Avoid

- Choosing too many goals
- Making daily tasks too big
- Skipping reflection
- Ignoring progress measurables
- Relying on motivation instead of systems
- Picking a theme that's too vague
- Trying to remake your whole life in 30 days

A great plan is small, specific, and repeatable.

Template You Can Reuse
"Create a 30-day plan with:

- theme
- weekly focus
- daily micro-actions
- reflection
- progress measures

Theme: [paste]."

Speed Tip
Add: "Now give me a one-page version."

The model will compress everything into a neat, printable layout.

Closing Thoughts — The 10-Hour Workweek Shift

A 10-hour savings each week is not an abstract promise. It's the cumulative effect of removing friction from dozens of routine decisions, tasks, and planning steps that normally consume attention.

Once those bottlenecks are stripped out, the shape of your workweek changes. You spend less time orienting yourself and more time acting with clarity.

Life After Friction

When daily tasks take less effort, the day feels less crowded. You spend fewer minutes deciding what to do next, rewriting the same emails, reorganizing your priorities, or piecing together information you've already seen. The reduction in cognitive load is noticeable. You stop managing your day reactively and start operating with a predictable rhythm.

Choosing the High-Leverage Path

The central shift isn't about working faster—it's about choosing better leverage. You offload steps that don't require your judgment, compress tasks that don't require your creativity, and systemize the parts of your life that repeat. This approach doesn't remove your involvement; it removes the inefficiency around your involvement. High-leverage work is anything that produces a clear outcome without requiring unnecessary attention.

What This Unlocks Next

Once the basic friction is gone, you create space for higher-value work and clearer thinking. You can direct more of your effort toward strategy, learning, relationships, writing, planning, and projects that benefit from your actual judgment. The result is not just saved time—it's a shift in how you allocate attention. A lighter cognitive load creates room for better decisions, deeper focus, and more consistent progress.

This book provides the prompts and systems that start that shift. What happens next comes from how you use the time and mental bandwidth you reclaim.

Appendix

Productivity & Focus (10 Prompts)

1. Daily Plan Builder

"Create my daily plan. Include priorities, schedule, and one focus block. Here are my tasks: [paste]."

2. Weekly Planning Blueprint

"Build my weekly plan with priorities, themes, and required outcomes. Context: [paste]."

3. Priority Clarifier

"Rank these tasks by impact, urgency, and effort. Tasks: [paste]."

4. Delegation Simulator

"Identify what I can delegate, automate, or eliminate from this list: [paste]."

5. Task Breakdown Tool

"Break this task into clear, small steps with estimated time. Task: [paste]."

6. Decision Helper

"Help me choose between these options. Pros, cons, risks, and recommendation: [paste]."

7. Email Triage

"Sort these emails into: reply, delegate, decide later, or ignore. Emails: [paste]."

8. Meeting Synthesis

"Summarize this meeting with decisions, owners, deadlines. Notes: [paste]."

9. 15-Minute Focus Booster
"Give me a 15-minute plan to move this task forward. Task: [paste]."

10. Energy-Aware Schedule Optimizer
"Create a schedule based on my current energy level: [low/medium/high]. Tasks: [paste]."

Communication & Writing (10 Prompts)

11. Email Reply Drafting
"Draft a concise, clear email reply. Tone: [tone]. Content: [paste]."

12. Rewrite for Tone
"Rewrite this text in [tone: professional, friendly, firm, concise]. Text: [paste]."

13. Clear & Concise Rewrite
"Rewrite this to be shorter, clearer, and easier to understand. Text: [paste]."

14. Difficult Conversation Coaching
"Help me communicate this difficult message effectively. Situation: [paste]."

15. Presentation Prep
"Turn this into a presentation outline with key points and flow. Topic: [paste]."

16. Bullet-to-Paragraph Expansion
"Expand these bullets into a coherent paragraph. Bullets: [paste]."

17. Paragraph-to-Bullet Compression
"Condense this text into bullet points. Text: [paste]."

18. Executive Summary Maker
"Create an executive summary of this material in 5 sentences. Content: [paste]."

19. Social Posts in My Voice
"Write 3 social posts in my tone: [describe tone]. Topic: [paste]."

20. Edit for Clarity & Flow
"Improve clarity, flow, and readability without changing meaning. Text: [paste]."

Work & Career (10 Prompts)

21. Strategy Simulator
"Give me strategic options for this situation with pros and risks. Context: [paste]."

22. Pros/Cons Analyzer
"Provide pros, cons, risks, and recommendation for these choices: [paste]."

23. Market Research Short Report
"Summarize this market with trends, problems, and opportunities. Industry: [paste]."

24. Policy Explainer
"Explain this policy in plain language with implications. Policy: [paste]."

25. Sales Page Draft
"Draft a sales page with problem, solution, features, and call-to-action. Product: [paste]."

26. Grant or Pitch Draft
"Create a compelling pitch or grant draft using: goal, need, impact, and ask. Details: [paste]."

27. Process Mapping
"Map this process step-by-step with owners and timing. Process: [paste]."

28. SOP Creation
"Write an SOP with purpose, steps, quality checks, and variations. Task: [paste]."

29. Workflow Simplification
"Identify steps to eliminate, automate, or combine in this workflow. Workflow: [paste]."

30. Meeting Agenda Builder
"Create a clear, outcome-focused agenda for this meeting. Topic: [paste]."

Personal Life (10 Prompts)

31. Meal Planning
"Create a week of meals based on these preferences and constraints: [paste]."

32. Grocery Automation
"Generate a grocery list with categories from this meal plan: [paste meals]."

33. Health Habit Tracking
"Build a simple habit tracker for sleep, movement, and nutrition. Goals: [paste]."

34. Sleep Optimization Notebook
"Summarize patterns and recommendations based on this sleep data: [paste]."

35. Vacation Planning

"Build a trip itinerary with activities, timing, and budget. Destination: [paste]."

36. Contractor Comparison
"Compare these contractors with strengths, risks, and recommendation. Info: [paste]."

37. Budget Snapshot
"Create a simple monthly budget snapshot with categories. Numbers: [paste]."

38. Gift Ideas
"Generate personalized gift ideas based on this person's interests: [paste]."

39. Family Communication Helper
"Draft clear messages for coordinating family plans. Topic: [paste]."

40. Memory-Capture Journaling
"Turn this moment or event into a short reflective journal entry. Details: [paste]."

Learning & Growth (10 Prompts)

41. Book Summary
"Summarize this book in key ideas, insights, and examples. Notes: [paste]."

42. Article Synthesis
"Extract the core argument and supporting points from this article. Link or text: [paste]."

43. Teach Me in My Learning Style
"Teach me this concept using my learning style. Style: [paste]. Topic: [paste]."

44. Micro-Course Creation
"Create a 5-lesson micro-course with objectives and exercises. Topic: [paste]."

45. Skill Roadmap
"Create a roadmap from beginner to advanced with milestones. Skill: [paste]."

46. Mistake Analysis
"Analyze this mistake: what happened, root cause, lessons, and next step. Details: [paste]."

47. Bias Checking
"Check this thinking for biases, alternative interpretations, and missing info. Situation: [paste]."

48. Data Interpretation
"Interpret this data: patterns, causes, missing context, and takeaway. Data: [paste]."

49. Insight Extraction
"Extract the core idea, why it matters, and practical application. Material: [paste]."

50. 30-Day Growth Plan
"Create a 30-day plan with weekly themes, daily micro-actions, and metrics. Goal: [paste].

Author's Note

These prompts were developed through direct testing with ChatGPT across dozens of real scenarios. They reflect what consistently saves time and reduces friction for everyday users.

Acknowledgements

Thank you to beta readers who tested early versions of these prompts in work, home, management, writing and planning.

Notes

Prompt behavior evolves as AI models update. The prompts here represent stable patterns that hold across current versions.

About the Author

Merritt Altman is a lifelong technology early adopter with more than twenty-five years of experience in public relations, information technology, and digital strategy. She helps readers integrate AI into daily life with clarity, practicality, and real-world application.

Other Books by Merritt Altman

Make and Master Your AI Twin

The AI Twin for Family History (with Anthony Brewer)

ChatGPT for writers (coming soon)

A Note from the Author

If these prompts made your days smoother or your workflow easier, a short review would mean a great deal. Your feedback helps the book reach others who need simple, practical AI guidance.

Thank you

Recommended Reading

Make and Master Your AI Twin

The AI Twin Workbook

Building a Second Brain with AI

Preview of *Make and Master Your AI Twin*

The following pages include a preview *from Make and Master Your AI Twin:*

Chapter 1—The Rise of the Digital Twin - From Industrial Tools to Personal Revolution

LET'S START AT THE beginning. What is an AI Twin? Better yet—let's begin with what it isn't.

You might imagine a video version of yourself: a talking digital replica that gives presentations, trains your team, or leads meetings while you're somewhere else. That technology does exist—but it's an evolution of the AI twin known as an avatar.

An avatar represents your appearance and voice.

An AI twin represents your mind—how you think, write, and decide.

Once you've mastered your AI twin, building a visual avatar becomes a natural next step. But before you create the face, you need the foundation—the thinking engine that makes it authentic.

In this section, we'll focus on that foundation: how to build and train your twin so it can improve your work, decisions, and daily life. The future forms—avatars, virtual agents, digital teachers—are up to you.

Meet Your Twin

We are entering an age where intelligence is no longer limited to biology. Every email you write, message you send, or note you take is now a fragment of language that can be converted to data. When combined, they form a pattern: you.

For the first time in human history, that pattern can be digitized, extended, and reactivated through artificial intelligence. Not as science fiction, but as an everyday tool.

It's no secret that we are more overloaded with information than ever before and yet underpowered in attention. Look at the number of self-help books on systems, procedures, and methods that promise to simplify your life (there are thousands). We spend our days reacting to alerts instead of creating meaning.

The AI twin can reverse that ratio.

It holds your place in the chaos, so you can return to thinking.

Understanding the Difference: AI Twins vs. Chatbots vs. Virtual Assistants

The coming era won't be defined by artificial intelligence alone. It will be defined by symbiotic intelligence—humans who can think with machines without losing themselves.

The AI twin is your first step into that world. Learn to master it, and you don't just automate tasks; you will extend the reach of human thought itself.

Your AI twin doesn't replace you; it enhances you. It extends your time, reach, and ability to be present in other areas instead of just answering emails or delegating tasks.

Simply put, it is a digital replica of your mind, trained on your unique writing style, personal habits, thought processes, and decision-making patterns. It will learn to think like you within the limits you set.

By providing it with your data, words, and goals, it will learn to think and respond as you do. While an assistant follows commands, a twin anticipates needs.

It combines two recent breakthroughs: the power of large language models, which can understand

and generate language at near-human levels, and persistent memory systems, which allow those models to “remember” who you are. Over time, through interaction and correction, it becomes a working simulation of how you process information and make decisions.

The twin is neither alive, conscious, nor emotional. It has no desires. It simply acts as a mirror: one that reflects your knowledge, personality, and style in a practical way. It doesn't feel or decide. However, when used effectively, it becomes more than just a mere reflection. It becomes a force multiplier for your intelligence.

www.ingramcontent.com/pod-product-compliance
Lightning Source LLC
LaVergne TN
LVHW090304210926
848480LV00001B/130
* 9 7 9 8 2 9 5 4 3 2 9 8 9 *